Birthflowers
of the LANDSCAPE™

Mystical Secrets to Year-Round Color in Your Garden

Linton Wright McKnight

COMMERCIAL PUBLISHING NETWORK
dedicated to ENVIRONMENTAL IMPROVEMENT

MILLEDGEVILLE, GEORGIA

Cover illustration copyright ©1998 by Jerry Tiritilli
Landscape architectural drawings copyright ©1998 by Jonathan D. Hutslar
Zone Map on page 22 courtesy of the Agriculture Research Service, USDA

SAN # 299-4666
Published by: Commercial Publishing Network
161 Swint Avenue, P. O. Box 1885-601
Milledgeville, Georgia 31061

Editorial direction by Katherine Buttler
Book and cover design by Karen E. Smith of Stateless Design, Atlanta

First Edition 10 9 8 7 6 5 4 3 2 1

ISBN 1-891401-09-2
McKnight, Linton Wright, 1942–
        Birthflowers of the Landscape : mystical secrets to year-round color in your garden. -- 1st ed.
            p.   cm.
        Includes bibliographical references (p.122) and index.
        ISBN 1-891401-09-2 (hardcover). — ISBN 1-891401-10-6 (softcover)
        1. Plants, Ornamental. 2. Landscape gardening. 3. Birthflowers.
    4. Color in gardening.   I. Title.
        SB407.M325   1994
635.9'53 — dc21   97-35367
                                                                    CIP

Printed in Hong Kong

*This book is dedicated to local government and civic leaders all across America
who see the value of "year-round color" in the public landscape and the local pride this generates
in our communities, as well as the role municipal compost plays in accomplishing it.
Without the help of these people in local government, who are willing to allocate funds
so that we might compost rather than bury yard wastes, our dream of color all year
would be much more difficult and would take much longer.*

(Photo courtesy of the U.S. Department of Agrigulture.)

❖CONTENTS❖

❧·FOREWORD·❧

HAVING KNOWN LIN MCKNIGHT since boyhood, growing up together in our native Milledgeville, Georgia, I have seen the passion he brings to the projects that are dear to his heart. Always a lover of flowering plants and landscaping, he has, in my opinion, written one of the best books ever to encourage people in their beginning journey to have, to desire, to collect, and to use flowering plants in their own landscape settings whether personal, residential, institutional, or communal.

Having myself been a commercial nurseryman, landscaper, and director of a botanical garden for the last 30 years, I have so often heard the comment from lay people that "I love plants, but I don't know where or how to get started" or "I love plants, but I don't have a green thumb." This impressive and lovingly written volume can change that common attitude after just the first few pages! As an easy to read and understand guidebook to begin what for so many of us has been a life-long labor of love, excitement, and fulfillment with plants, this beautifully crafted book is the perfect inspiration for turning those black thumbs out there into a decidedly more pleasant shade of green.

People who have made growing and collecting plants the love of their lives will steadfastly agree with Lin that getting involved personally with plants and their culture will enrich your life, beautify your private surroundings and your whole community, provide insights into living a better, more peaceful and graceful lifestyle that will make you happier, and even steadily increase the value of your property. What a powerful combination! The simply elegant concepts and ideas outlined in the following pages should be a great first step for anyone seeking the joy of that elusive green thumb!

H. D. EDWARDS
DIRECTOR, LOCKERLY ARBORETUM
MILLEDGEVILLE, GEORGIA

Nomenclature

OF THE BIRTHFLOWERS OF THE LANDSCAPE™

 To understand the classification and nomenclature of the Birthflowers used in this book, simply refer to the following chart. The genus name of the plant is the correct Birthflower name, however, due to common usage, three of the Birthflowers—the daylily, crape myrtle, and azalea—are referred to by their common name. Though each genus has many species and countless cultivated varieties, they are not included in this chart.

Month	Birthflower of the Landscape™	Family	Genus	Common Name
January	Narcissus	Amaryllis	Narcissus	Daffodil
February	Forsythia	Olive	Forsythia	Golden Bells
March	Azalea	Heath	Rhododendron	Azalea
April	Iris	Iris	Iris	Flag
May	Rose	Rose	Rose	Rose
June	Hydrangea	Saxifrage	Hydrangea	Hydrangea
July	Crape Myrtle	Loosestrife	Lagerstroemia	Crape Myrtle
August	Phlox	Phlox	Phlox	Garden Phlox
September	Canna	Canna	Canna	Canna Lily
October	Daylily	Lily	Hemerocallis	Daylily
November	Chrysanthemum	Composite	Chrysanthemum	Mum
December	Camellia	Tea	Camellia	Japonica

Commercial Landscaping Network (CLN) is a wholesale flower/giftware business that, while selling to the retail market and involving itself in civic-oriented causes, remains focused on its dedication to environmental improvement, especially in the areas of composting and aesthetic landscaping. We welcome any correspondence.

Disclaimer Although every effort has been made to make this book as accurate as possible, there may be mistakes both typographical and horticultural. Much of the mystique information offered herein is based on my observations. The taxonomy and classification of the plant kingdom cannot only be complicated, but because of everyday usage it is constantly changing. Locational conditions of temperature, humidity, altitude, hours of sunlight, soil condition, and many other factors cause plants to grow and bloom at different times. For these reasons, this book should be used only for general information and not as the last word in horticulture and botany. The publisher and author shall have no liability or responsibility to any person or entity regarding any loss or damage caused either directly or indirectly by the information contained herein. If this is not agreeable to you, you may return this book to the publisher for a full refund.

This book represents the opinions and beliefs of the author only, and I remain solely responsible for its content. I have made statements and recommendations drawn from experience, research, and knowledge, and believe them to be correct. However, I welcome and wholeheartedly encourage any corrections and comments from any reader, especially those comments that will improve the next edition of *Birthflowers of the Landscape*. Please direct them to me at: 161 Swint Avenue, Milledgeville, Georgia, 31061.

❧ PREFACE ❧

Flowers worthy of Paradise.

JOHN MILTON

WHILE WORKING IN MY LANDSCAPE BUSINESS over the years, I have been astonished at how little attention and emphasis is placed on the season of bloom of beautiful and showy landscape plants. As a result of my interest in the tangible, vibrant beauty of flowers, as well as the elusive, yet palpable qualities that forge a connection between us and our flowers, I wrote this book focused on a basic concept of "color all year." When each of these 12 Birthflowers is obtained for your yard or windowsill, and you are careful in that selection, then it is easy to have color all year and have a flower that will magically bloom on or near your birthday! But I also want people to recognize and appreciate how connected we are to our own Birthflowers, and so this book goes beyond the simple caretaking of plants.

Each month has its "Birthflower," and each Birthflower of the Landscape™ has a special meaning—a symbolic association to enrich your life. These flowers are rather like birthstones in that each has traditional personifications of people born in their season of bloom. You may have noticed that the jewelry business does a rather fine job of promoting "birthstones," which are very popular birthday gifts worldwide. Unfortunately, the landscape industry is not as successful with, or vocal about Birthflowers, which is a shame. How thoroughly fulfilling it is to have a living thing turn more beautiful about the same time you celebrate your special day!

This book seeks to enlighten the general populace on what their Birthflowers are and how to care for them. Each flower has been carefully selected according to its season of bloom, ease of growth, cold hardiness, and vibrant color. You have to plant them only once, and every following year they will bloom and look even more magnificent than the year before. This permanence makes them the perfect backdrop for small plantings of annuals. In fact, all of the primary features of Birthflowers make them ideal for your year-round landscape, to provide beauty and pleasure . . . enduring enough to last a lifetime.

For many people, nature has a spiritual dimension. I myself feel renewed, strengthened, and recommitted to life when I immerse myself in nature. What better place to do that than in a garden, particularly one that you have created for yourself, one you have grown literally from the ground up?

When I am able to leave the noise, corruption, and discord of the city for a while and give myself up to the harmony and rhythm of nature, I come back to my home strengthened and renewed—mentally, physically, emotionally. The plants displayed within these pages have helped millions of people in the same way. And by gardeners following the basic care suggestions outlined in this book, these wonderful plants will perhaps help millions more to express themselves through the spiritual dimension of nature.

It is through observation of personality traits and how people perceive themselves, combined and connected with attributes of flowers that the "Mystique" section of this book was developed. Throughout history, connections have been made between the human spirit and physical phenomena. An ancient philosopher once compared human courage to jade in much the same way as this book sees evidence of courage in the April Birthflower, the Iris.

It is a widely held belief, and one to which I subscribe, that whatever the human mind embraces as possible, it can achieve. Vital mental renewal is the result of education, continually honoring and expanding the mind. Becoming aware of character strengths through association with a personal birthflower can be a first step in a process of self-knowledge and growth.

LINTON WRIGHT McKNIGHT

❧INTRODUCTION❧

God Almighty first planted a garden.

FRANCIS BACON

PERENNIALS ARE PLANTS that, with a little care, will return each and every year looking better and better. My main objective in creating this book is to show how a yard can have color year round with perennials. A garden, regardless of its size, that is well-tended and loved will abound with hues of the rainbow, but it is about more than color. I will introduce to you a deeper connection to the garden you cultivate and perhaps give you ideas to improve on what you already have.

A garden reflects the personalities of those people associated with its individual flowers; the strengths of people are represented in amazing ways in the flowers you grow. Have you ever noticed how eagerly Narcissus, the first flower of the new year and the January Birthflower, thrusts itself from earth? Now look at your friends who are born in January. The traits that so tangibly define the Narcissus—ambitious, rational, responsible—are visible in those people who are January born. You will be surprised, as you read through the descriptions of each Birthflower, to find and recognize many loved ones in these pages, simply by virtue of their connection with their Birthflower. In addition, I will bring to you the secrets of your personal association and connection with your Birthflower, the flower of the month in which you were born.

Each chapter gives you the genus of a plant, a cultivar (cultivated variety) of which can be found to bloom naturally during the designated month in most parts of the northern hemisphere. Historical anecdotes, legends, and tidbits lead off each chapter. Flowers existed before written records, and the chapters recount popular stories that are entertaining, colorful, and serve to show that flowers have captured the attention and imagination of man for millennia.

Flowers transcend cultures and civilizations. In their passage through time they have acquired importance to man in several areas: commerce, food, art, religion, medicine, and folklore. Flowers have gained their own "personalities" throughout the ages and now we can recognize and establish our connection to the flower that blooms most closely to the time of year of our birth. Each Birthflower chapter continues with the "Mystique" section of the flower and its month, with human interest and personality traits attached to each. Read your Birthflower synopsis carefully and compare its traits to your own—you'll be pleasantly surprised.

The more pragmatic, helpful "Culture" section of each chapter tells how the plants are classified botanically and gives examples of different species within the genus of the plant, species you are probably familiar with and didn't know belong together. For example, the genera Crocus, Freesia, Gladiolus, and Iris all belong in the Iris family (Iridaceae), with the Iris genus containing more than 200 Iris species!

Also included in this section are suggestions from the author, "Gardening Tips"—highlights of each plant's needs rather than a comprehensive manual—on how to help your plants thrive in your particular yard. You will find out how and where to plant certain flowers and what common insect and disease problems might threaten them. You will learn water requirements, pruning techniques, and propagation methods for each Birthflower—vital information if you want to get your plants to multiply heartily. If you seek further information on these plants, we have included a bibliography. For new gardeners, our Glossary is a nice quick reference tool to use as you come across unfamiliar gardening terms in this book.

Finally, in the "Availability" section of each chapter, we tell you when to look for these plants on the market in general. Specifically, our pricing and order forms in the back of the book will tell you where you can get the best wholesale deal on these plants from us (along with other gift ideas). In addition, we give the address and phone number of a society dedicated to that particular Birthflower.

Regardless of whether you are a beginner or a more experienced gardener, building your garden around Birthflowers of the Landscape™ will provide a foundation for an expanding experience of color. Don't be satisfied trying to experiment with two or three plants. Buy and properly plant enough of a variety to make a show. You can easily have magnificent color from your garden all year long utilizing these twelve gorgeous Birthflowers of the Landscape™.

A few Landscaping Principles
TO GET YOU STARTED

Ever charming, ever new,
When will the landscape tire the view?

JOHN DYER

Designing and Planning Your Landscape

Without a plan, you are lost. Though one can get a doctorate in Landscape Architecture and spend a lifetime pondering the elements of design, it is easier and much more enjoyable to learn and practice a few important techniques. You must set priorities and long-range goals. What do you want your garden to be? You probably want your garden to be an expression of your own personality and way of life. In addition you will likely be concerned with low maintenance, visual appeal, and privacy.

The first task is to get your wants and needs down on paper. Design an overall sense of personal place, an area with a presence about it. Mark the area where walls and fences are needed for privacy. Is there room in the budget for structures (such as statues, gazebos, etc.), fountains, night lighting, and irrigation? Select a focal point and concentrate on it. Perhaps you will select a specimen plant or tree, a water fountain, a fence, a bench, or even a small attractive birdhouse.

Plant nothing without a reason. A deciduous shade tree planted about 15 feet from, and on the southeast or southwest side of a house could save as much in utility bills as the cost of your whole garden. (The shade from the tree in summer helps you save on air-conditioning costs; in the winter, the leafless tree will allow sun's heat to reach your house.) Replacing high maintenance grass with flowering shrubs can save a great deal in both time and money. Color, form, texture, and staged height are all important considerations in choices of plants and in the planting itself.

For added interest and variety, try building small berms, or mounds. Soil for these berms can be obtained by edging around walks, drives, and curbs on your property. Just dig a small six-inch wide and four-inch deep trench along the edge of these boundary markings and use the soil collected for mounding your berm. The resulting trench forms a definitive border or edging with attractive eye appeal and easy maintenance when laid out in large sweeping "S" curves and "C" curves. These are important additions to overall garden shape, but squiggling lines are distracting. Remember to plant in groups, in both colors and plant variety. Your garden or yard will be more interesting if it is not planted in long straight lines and if plants are not repetitively alternated. Planting in odd numbers such as three, five, or seven is a good principle to follow.

Planting plants too closely together is one of the most common mistakes in gardening. Give each plant enough room for its mature size. Its roots need air; circulating air can alleviate bug and rot problems. In addition, allow plenty of space between groups of plants for best appearance and for expansion room.

Keep in mind that most perennials will bloom only about two weeks each year. Having color year round in your garden will require some thought and effort. For example, become familiar with what blooms when and arrange the plants according to your tastes. Patience, time, and growth are all required, for your garden is never really finished. It takes several years for a garden to fully mature, and it needs your guidance: For example, the Rose has several species that flower at different times during the summer, so by planting several of them (or the right combination) you can have rose blossoms all summer.

If your budget does not allow you to plant everything in one season, divide the plant material you think you'll need into thirds and buy/plant it over three years. The following selection of plant material will give the longest season of bloom and will grow bigger and more beautiful every year with a minimum amount of effort. A typical plan might look something like this:

PLANT NAME	YEAR 1 PLANTING	YEAR 2 PLANTING	YEAR 3 PLANTING
Narcissus	15		
Forsythia		3	
Azalea			5
Iris	15		
Rose		3	
Hydrangea			5
Crape Myrtle		3	
Phlox			7
Canna	3		
Daylily	15		
Chrysthanthemum			7
Camellia		3	

SAMPLE LANDSCAPE—BEFORE

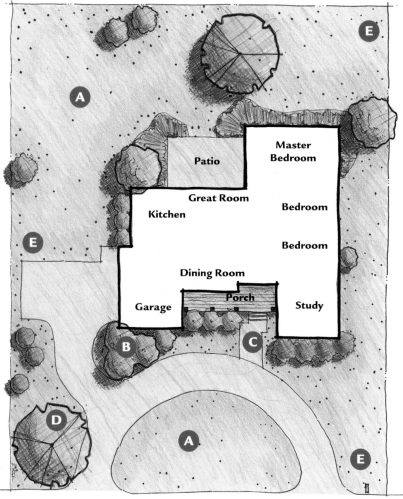

NOTES:

A. Flat landscape with no composition (no color).

B. House is hidden and dwarfed by overgrown shrubs (appears dark and drab; cannot look out windows and light cannot come into house).

C. House is not framed with a focus on the entrance.

D. Shade tree at the left is too low to the ground (needs to be limbed up to 7' to 8' off of the ground).

E. No sense of "place."

SAMPLE LANDSCAPE—AFTER

NOTES:

A. Landscape has character, composition and unity.

B. House is opened up, framed and allowed to breath.

C. Entrance is inviting.

D. High maintenance grass is replaced by shrubs and perennials which provide year-long color.

E. Addition of shade trees and evergreen trees provide a sense of "place" and anchor the house to the property.

F. Shade tree on the left is limbed up to 7' to 8' off of the ground.

G. Overgrown shrubs are either pruned to tree-form or drastically pruned (a task best performed in March) to the appropriate size.

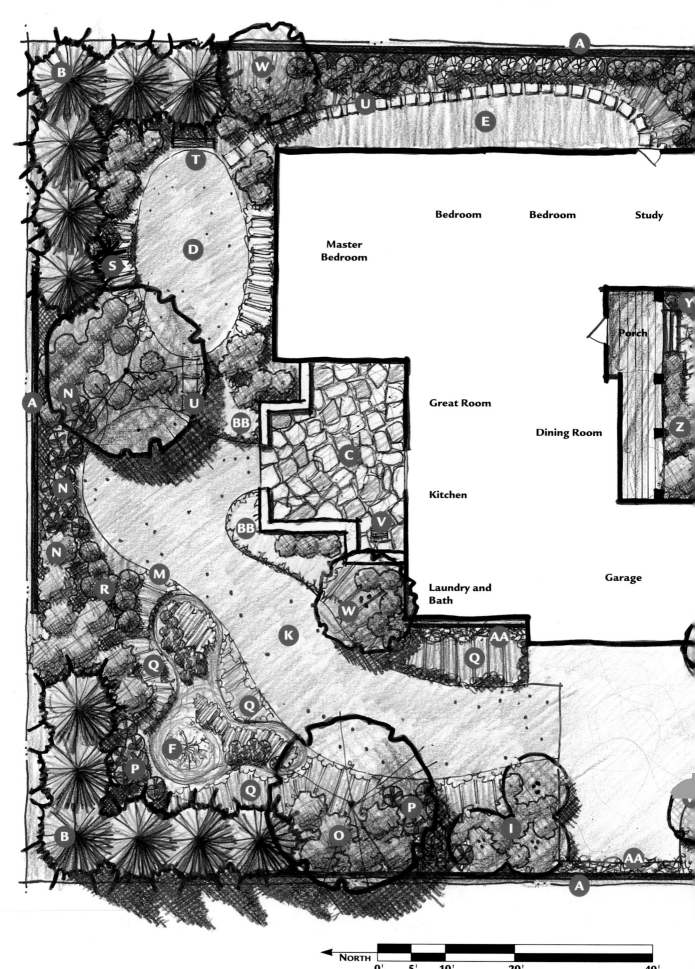

Master
Bedroom

Bedroom   Bedroom   Study

Great Room

Porch

Dining Room

Kitchen

Garage

Laundry and
Bath

NORTH
0'   5'   10'   20'   40'

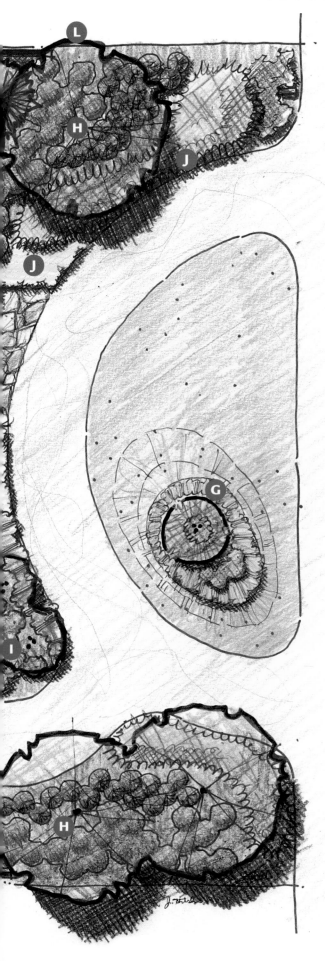

NOTES:

A. Privacy fence (for enclosure, screening and sound attenuation).

B. (12) Tall evergreen trees for screening and spatial definition.

C. Stone patio/entertainment area enclosed by 18" seatwall.

D. Azalea and Iris* Garden outside master bedroom— a formal garden in part shade; (23) Azaleas and Iris*.

E. View Garden outside bedrooms & study (with (19) Camellia, (11) Canna and Phlox* in part shade; a stepping stone path connects the study with the Azalea/Iris Garden).

F. Water Garden: pond and fountain with (19) water-loving Canna & Iris* (a focal point in part shade that also provides sound attenuation).

G. Planted berm with (1) tree-form Crape Myrtle, Daylily*, Chrysanthemum*, Iris* and Narcissus* (in full sun): to screen streetside view of garage area and provide depth to the landscape.

H. (27) Hydrangea, (21) Camellia and Daylily* in overlapping groups of contrasting color and height (in part shade; in groups of the same color).

I. (9) Azalea under shrubs pruned to tree-form (in part shade)

J. Entry color scheme: Narcissus* and Phlox* together in the middle by entrance with Daylily* to the right and Iris* to the left; planted in groups of the same color for boldness.

K. Grass area (open/living space that is lower in maintenance than before)

L. Large shade tree on southeast corner of house (to shade house when mature, saving on utility bills)

M. Large, swooping "S-curve" (edged to define between grass and planting bed; soft curves are easy to mow)

N. (8) Forsythia, (13) Canna and (10) Hydrangea along fence in background (with plenty of room for mature size)

O. (6) Forsythia in background (in part shade)

P. (16) Canna in Background (in part shade)

Q. Phlox* (in part shade)

R. (7) Camellia (to frame the water garden; in part shade)

S. Statue (for interest)

T. Bench (for reflection)

U. Stepping Stones

V. Grill (located next to the kitchen and out of the way)

W. Overgrown shrub pruned as a tree

X. Evergreen tree (to separate two different spaces)

Y. (4) Roses (in full sun)

Z. (7) Chrysanthemum (in full sun)

AA. (3) Espaliered Roses on fence or structure (in full sun)

BB. Narcissus* (in part shade)

* The quantity of Narcissus, Phlox, Iris, Daylilies, and Chrysanthemums depends on the spacing used at planting.

FOR BEST RESULTS, THESE PLANTS SHOULD BE PLANTED IN SOIL THAT HAS BEEN TILLED AND AMENDED PROPERLY.

And because the breath of flowers is far sweeter in the air (where it comes and goes, like the warbling of music) than in the hand, therefore nothing is more fit for that delight than to know what be the flowers and plants that do best perfume the air.

FRANCIS BACON

Delightful Benefits of Your Birthflower Garden

As you begin your garden you will find unexpected benefits to delight you. Gardening is one of the healthiest things one can do, both mentally and physically. For stress control and anxiety release, there is nothing more relaxing than working outside in the garden, sitting on the ground, digging and plowing with your hands in the earth, placing plants, seeds, or cuttings where before there was emptiness. Americans are becoming more aware—from friends, doctors, media—of the body's ability to heal itself, and preventative medicine is widely practiced today. The time and energy spent in both the planning and planting stages of gardening allow for the relief of the stress of our hectic lives. It is widely accepted today that billions of dollars in stress-related medical costs could be saved if more Americans practiced gardening regularly.

The exercise you get is also one of the best weight-loss programs available anywhere. Personal fitness is on the minds of many of us today, and we are looking for enjoyable ways of exercising to stay trim or to return to our former youthful appearance. Good health requires a program of activity, and the exercise you get from gardening can help you lose weight and stay fit. Because gardening requires the use of all the major muscle groups, firmer muscle tone and increased strength are added bonus benefits.

Another surprising bonus is that what you do for your mental and physical health can probably benefit you financially as well in the long run. Studies made by the National Association of Realtors reveal that properly landscaped homes will bring 20 percent more in resale value than those that are not. A $5,000 investment in landscaping on a $100,000 home will return you $20,000 at the time of resale—quite a return for your investment. As incredible as that sounds, it is possible; especially if you are able to enjoy the beauty of your yard and all of the other pride of ownership benefits in the meantime! To learn more of the mental and physical benefits of gardening, contact: The American Horticultural Therapy Association, 362-A Christopher Avenue, Gaithersburg, Maryland, 20879; phone (301) 869-2397.

Taking Care of Your Birthflowers of the Landscape™

Once you have finished your landscape plan, you are ready to plant. Be careful, though. Ironically, the most important part of the planting process is often the most neglected. For success in planting, it is essential that root systems get the proper amount of water and the soil be friable (see Glossary). This is most easily done by adding and mixing compost into the soil. Many gardeners ignore this step altogether and are surprised when their garden is less fruitful than they had hoped.

Compost is nothing more than the biological reduction of organic wastes to humus, a brown substance of decayed organic matter. Organic matter such as leaves, sticks, chipped wood, and even food scraps that have gone through a heating and digesting process makes the best soil additive and the best mulching material. Peat moss and ground pine bark work almost as well as a soil additive, and pine straw and many other materials work almost as well as a mulch.

Composting will happen naturally to a pile of leaves that is left alone for 4 years or more, but can be made to happen in 4 months when the leaf pile is mixed, aerated by turning, and watered down when dry. Start your own compost pile (in fact, many catalogs and garden centers sell specialized compost containers for individual homes) and encourage your local politicians to compost municipal trash. For example, the state of Georgia has mandated exclusion of yard wastes in landfills. This is a vital step in communities beginning to take charge of their own composting.

When mixed 50-50 or even 25-75 percent with soil from the planting hole or tilled into the planting area, compost works like magic. It makes clay soils drain better, sandy soils hold water longer, and makes both soils more fertile. For these reasons, plant survival rate is dramatically improved. It might be difficult to accept this, but you should be willing to spend as much money on compost—used as both a soil additive and a mulch—as you spend on your plant material!

Mixing humus with soil may sound easy, but actually doing it takes a great deal of physical effort. Just as your plan is good mental exercise, this important mixing step is good physical exercise. This is one reason gardening is such good therapy. It helps you lose weight and stay in good health, while at the same time giving you pride and satisfaction in your work.

Most ornamental plants perform best with a neutral pH, a 7 on a scale from 1 to 14. The potential of Hydrogen (pH) level can be raised (made more alkaline) by adding lime and can be lowered (made more acidic) by adding sulfur. It is better to remember that when there is an abundant supply of humus, plants are less dependent on a specific soil pH.

You should know that there is just as much to a plant under the ground and invisible to you as there is above the ground. It is this underground element that is the most important to the plant's survival. In winter, when the top of the plant is dormant, the roots still continue to grow, so if you decide to transplant, do it in October or November. This will give the roots several months to become established in the soil at a time when there is less demand on them from the rest of the plant. They can concentrate on becoming healthy without having to feed and nurture the part of the plant that remains above ground. Remember to loosen and cut pot-bound roots when removing the plant from a container. When planting bare-root plants, add a chemical root stimulator.

The most common transplanting error is the tendency most of us have to plant too deep. Roots need air as well as water and can get it only near the soil's surface. Keep in mind that a hole with a very large circumference—where roots can spread out, not just down—is most important. Where depth is concerned, plant only to the depth the plant was growing before, no deeper.

Water is the reason most plants die in your care. Either too little or too much water will cause trouble. Avoid planting in boggy areas. Most plants need a humus-rich, well-drained soil in order to thrive and become vibrant and healthy. Be sure to water well immediately after planting, every other day for a week, and then once a week for two months after that, provided it doesn't rain. Push your finger into the soil beside the plant: Add water if it isn't moist. Mulch (explained below) well to maintain even moisture.

Mulch has many uses in the landscape and its importance cannot be overstated. It keeps plant roots moist, makes it difficult for weeds to grow, and is visually attractive.

Compost is the best mulching material, but many other substances (such as pine straw, pine bark, pecan hulls, old chipped wood—something indigenous to your area) will do about as well and may be more accessible. Place mulch about four to six inches deep so that it will settle to about two to four inches. Do not allow any of the material to touch the main plant stem; it might cause stem rot, and that wound is easy access for insect and disease problems.

Watering, weeds, and insects are the three most troublesome things about gardening, and mulch is the easiest and the best combatant for all three. Mulching retains moisture around the plant and keeps it healthy—and a healthy plant is a poor target for bugs. Mulch also helps the plant maintain an even temperature, allows air to get to surface roots, and has great fertilizer qualities. A thick layer of mulch makes it hard for weed seeds to get established.

In the appearance of your garden, mulch offers another benefit: It just plain looks good. Its dark color allows for the establishment of good, strong, contrasting lines in the landscape and makes broad sweeping curves for prominent visual features. However, newly chipped wood might rob much needed nitrogen from your plants, so compost it before applying.

Mulching and pruning are the first steps to take in renovating a landscape. The first rule in pruning is: Don't leave a stub. When you prune close to the next main stem the plant can heal the wound. If you leave a stub, the plant cannot heal. Instead, it will eventually decay and leave a hole whereby insects and diseases can work their way into the plant.

Whenever you prune, new growth is stimulated somewhere on the plant within about 6 inches of the cut. This is the main reason most pruning should be confined to March and April. Otherwise, this new growth might freeze and die, weakening the whole plant.

Remove all dead and diseased wood. Keep an eye out for branches that rub together. The resulting wound might become a point of entry for insect and disease problems, so remove one of the rubbing branches. Allow each plant its own space so that it is not crowded by adjacent ones.

Pruning and mulching show the most immediate dramatic effect on a mature landscape. Mature plantings are very valuable and irreplaceable, and their appearance can easily be enhanced with a little thought and effort. Give them their own space by removing unwanted material or obstacles, even if this means removing another mature plant.

After flowering, most plants produce seeds. Seed production takes a lot of energy from the plant. To conserve this energy for healthier plants, cut off dead blooms (deadhead). Doing this also makes the whole garden look better, with unwanted brown blooms, stems, and foliage gone.

The flowers pictured in this book cover a wide range of landscaping features, such as sun and shade requirements. Study the following chart to become familiar with them.

FLOWER	DIVIDE TO PROPAGATE	SUN	PART SHADE	SHADE	EVERGREEN	SMALL TREE	SHRUB HERB/ MINI-SHRUB	BULB	COLOR
AZALEA			•		•		•		●●●●●●
CAMELLIA			•		•	•	•		●●●
CANNA	•	•	•					•	●●●●
CHRYSANTHEMUM	•	•	•				•		●●●●●●
CRAPE MYRTLE		•	•			•			●●●
DAYLILY	•	•	•					•	●●●●
FORSYTHIA		•	•				•		●●
HYDRANGEA			•						●●●
IRIS	•	•	•					•	●●●●
NARCISSUS	•	•	•	•				•	●●●
PHLOX	•	•	•				•		●●●●
ROSE		•	•			•	•		●●●●

Light Requirements
SUN means a full 8 hours of direct sunlight.

PART SHADE means 3–4 hours of direct sunlight.

SHADE means little or no direct sunlight.

Most plants will respond to receiving a little more direct sunlight than suggested with more bloom and better color.

October and November are the best times of the year to plant because the roots have all winter to strengthen before great demands are placed on them by the rest of the plant. Problems arise in northern areas when planting too near to the first freeze — the plants are literally heaved from the ground. Plant well enough in advance and mulch well to avoid this disaster, or wait until spring.

The bulbs and herbs shown here are easily propagated by division. With your hands, simply break up large clumps of plants into individual plants. If your neighbor has a crowded garden, offer to divide some of his or her prolific plants and ask if you can help yourself to some of the divided plants. This thinning of the garden will improve the aesthetic quality of your neighbor's garden and will give you a jump start on getting mature plants established in your own garden.

We all know that most plants growing in Alaska will not survive in Arizona. Humidity and altitude variables are difficult to assess. In an attempt to designate the areas in which specific plants will thrive, the U.S. Department of Agriculture has devised a Plant Hardiness Zone Map (page 22) which shows general areas of cold temperatures, the lower numbers on the map being the colder areas. A plant will normally survive and thrive in several zone areas south of the plant's designated zone or zones with higher numbers than the plant's designated zone numbers.

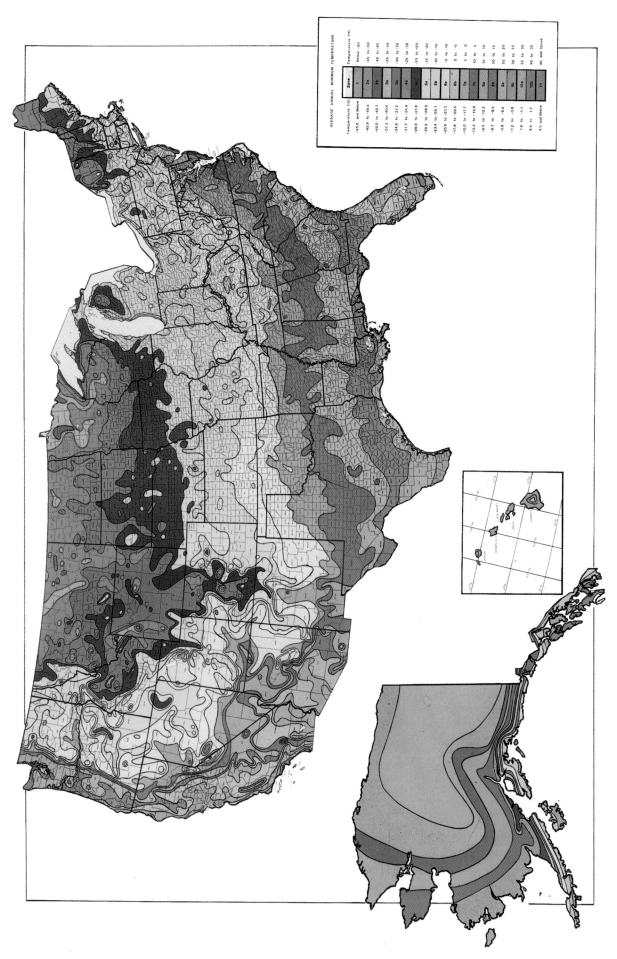

NOTES:

❖NARCISSUS❖
January Birthflower of the Landscape™

He that has two cakes of bread, let him sell one of them for some flowers of the Narcissus, for bread is food for the body, but Narcissus is food for the soul.

MOHAMMED

ONE OF THE OLDEST CULTIVATED flowering plants, the Narcissus was used many centuries ago by the ancient Egyptians for funeral wreaths, and today, 3,000 years later, the preserved remains are still recognizable as once-vivid blossoms. Originating in the areas of Spain and Portugal in prehistoric times, the Narcissus eventually spread to the shores of the Mediterranean and into the Middle East. These heralders of early spring were growing eagerly in gardens hundreds of years before the birth of Jesus.

Narcissus is Latin for daffodil, and the two words are interchangeable, with Narcissus being the formal botanical term for the genus of these members of the Amaryllis family. The name Narcissus is derived from the Greek word *narké*, meaning to benumb, referring to the narcotic quality of the flower's fragrance, which has a soothing influence on the nervous system. Thus it was used in ancient Greece to encourage

(Photo courtesy of Michael A. Dirr, Ph.D.)

sleep and to calm those suffering from hysteria. The Greeks, like the Egyptians, also sent loved ones on to the afterlife with the Narcissus, placing the bulbs and flowers in the coffins. Perhaps the most famous story of this flower is the Greek myth of Narcissus, a beautiful boy who, as punishment for rejecting a would-be lover, saw his own image reflected in a stream, fell in love with it, fell in the water, and drowned. In his place a Narcissus flower sprouted on the bank.

In 1862 an English gentleman named Peter Barr—known as the King of Daffodils due to his tireless and successful efforts to promote the flower—set up an ambitious syndicate to buy the collections of two ardent amateur English botanists. In doing so he undoubtedly saved the collections from completely disappearing. This responsible act in a large part made possible today's continually increasing cultivar registrations (which now average a hundred and sixty a year) coming from countries as diverse as the United States, Latvia, Great Britain, Hungary, Canada, Australia, Holland, and New Zealand.

The January/Narcissus
MYSTIQUE

**Ambitious
Rational
Responsible**

Being one of the early messengers of spring and one of the easiest flowers to grow has ensured the Narcissus's place as one of the most popular of all spring-flowering bulbs in America. The enthusiasm generated by gardening amateurs and professionals alike that has ignited a world-wide passion for this cool-weather flower is typically characteristic of January personalities. The ambition of those born with the flowering Narcissus leads them toward zealous pursuit of their goals. However, on balance, their rational, logical nature gives them a solid base in life. Similarly, the daffodil is dependable, and each bulb can be relied upon to sprout up again year after year. January born individuals are recognized as very responsible and not at all capricious by those who know them.

The Narcissus embodies many of these energetic traits in its eager thrust through the cold earth each year. To many, this lovely flower has become the dependable sign of hope in an otherwise bleak winter landscape. It is the reliable reminder that the warmer, brighter days of spring are not far away.

If you have a January birthday, planting these bulbs or forcing their early bloom in your home will serve to remind you of the strength of the traits you possess. These blossoms can spur you on to further develop this potential. Through a gift of Narcissus, you can encourage these solid aspects of your friends' personalities as well. You may wish to send an arrangement of fresh-cut blossoms or elegant silk flowers, which are beautiful, lively representations of this winter birthflower. Or perhaps you would rather give the bulbs themselves to be either planted in a garden or forced in an attractive dish inside. Whatever way you choose to share the Narcissus with those you love, you will be encouraging in them the development of the positive character traits of the January birthday flower.

(Photo courtesy of Michael A. Dirr, Ph.D.)

Culture

Zone 4

pH 6.0-7.5

Sun/Part Shade

The Amaryllis family has about 90 genera or subgroups, including Allium, Amaryllis, Galanthus, Hymenocallis (spider lily), and Narcissus. The 26 or so Narcissus species (also known by their common names of daffodil, paperwhite, or jonquil) have many hundreds of cultivars. They are native to Europe and the Mediterranean, and most are perfumed.

Height:
4 inches to 24 inches

Three popular divisions of Narcissus (out of eleven) are:

- Trumpet Narcissus has a large trumpet-shaped corona, stalks 16 to 20 inches tall, and flowers 3 to 4 inches wide that bloom early to mid spring. Unsurpassable is yellow in color, and Mount Hood is white.
- Large-cupped Narcissus has a slightly smaller corona, stalks 14 to 20 inches tall, and flowers up to $4^1/_2$ inches wide. Carlton is yellow and Ice Follies is white.
- Tazetta Narcissus has very fragrant flowers up to $1^1/_4$ inches wide in clusters of 4 to 8, stalks 18 inches tall, and sometimes blooms at Christmas (or earlier) in the South. Paperwhite is white, while Geranium is white with an orange cup and blooms in late spring.

Gardening TIPS

Growing
- These flowers easily naturalize and are trouble free in well-drained ground. They will grow anywhere except in waterlogged clay.
- Plant bulbs in the fall in humus-filled soil to a depth about three times their diameter, usually 6 inches apart and 6 inches deep in a well-drained, sunny spot.
- Fertilize with bonemeal.
- These flowers have no insect or disease problems.
- To get January bloom where snow is on the ground, they can be forced (made to bloom) (see Glossary) inside on a container of soil just by keeping them moist and in a sunny window until blooms begin to show.

Many seasoned gardeners will tell you to do as author Vita Sackville-West (1892-1962), creator of the famous garden at Sissinghurst in England, did. She liked to scatter Narcissus bulbs in the area she wanted them to grow, and would plant the bulbs exactly where they fell, ensuring a natural look when the flowers bloomed.

Pruning
- Deadhead (see Glossary) the plants by removing old blooms.
- Do not cut foliage because it is needed to produce the food for next year's blooms.
- Yellowing foliage can be hidden by adjacent plantings of Daylilies or Irises.

Galahad. (Photo courtesy of Hubert Bourne.)

Above: *(Photo courtesy of Michael A. Dirr, Ph.D.)* **Opposite:** ***Loch Brora.*** *(Photo courtesy of Hubert Bourne.)*

Propagation

- Allowing the leaves to die and fade naturally will feed the plant's bulb and will ensure flowers for next year.
- Divide (see Glossary) the plants after leaves fade in the spring.
- In order to get the largest blooms possible, divide groups of Narcissus every 3 to 5 years, and plant the bulbs about 6 inches deep.

Availability

OF JANUARY BIRTHFLOWER OF THE LANDSCAPE™

As with most flowers that will survive in most regions, Narcissus's outside blooms will come about a month later in the North than in the South (see Zone Map, page 22). Though some varieties are found growing outside in the South, obviously they are not likely to punch through the snow in a northern winter. To be forced inside, some Narcissus require about four months of cold storage in coolers. Forcing (see Glossary) January blooms inside can be a challenge for the home gardener. But we're in luck! Paperwhite Narcissus requires no cooling, blooming four to six weeks after adding water.

An especially nice single daffodil we recommend is the yellow daffodil, Carlton. It is beautiful, naturalizes so very well, freely reproduces over a wide part of the country, and it is an early bloomer, fragrant, and disease resistant. However, these flowers are especially nice when planted in large groups and in several colors. We offer an assortment of Narcissus so you can plant a variety together. Since Narcissus bulbs have a small window of opportunity for purchase and planting, and often quantities are limited, it would be wise for you to order about two months early (mid-July). Shipping generally runs from mid-September to mid-January, but supplies of the most popular varieties are frequently gone by mid-December.

It is our opinion that a single bulb does nothing for the garden. It merely looks accidental, so order bulbs in packages of at least 5. See order form for pricing.

To meet other people with an interest in NARCISSUS, *contact:*

American Daffodil Society, Inc.
1686 Gray Fox Trails
Milford, OH 45150-1521
(513) 248-9137

CHAPTER II

❧ FORSYTHIA ❧

February Birthflower of the Landscape™

The forsythia blossoms as a first sign of spring
But its soul still whispers of winter. . . .

JACQUELINE HAUN

NATIVE TO KOREA, Forsythia, a flowering shrub popular today in temperate gardens, is named for William Forsyth, a 16th-century gentleman famous in England for his keen intelligence and deep involvement in horticulture. A friendly man who was one of the seven founding members of the Horticulture Society of London (today the Royal Horticultural Society), Forsyth was for thirteen years the Curator of Chelsea Physic Garden as well as gardener to King George III.

Before his death in 1804, the famous Director of the Royal Gardens at Kensington Palace left a mixed legacy to his country: In addition to his contributions to gardening, this intelligent botanist had bluffed Parliament into paying £1500 for his invention of "Forsyth's Plaister" which was supposed to cure tree decay. Whether this mixture of soap and ash actually worked was the crux of a bitter controversy that lasted even after his death, and this independent man's legacy has outlived that of any of the members of the Parliament of his day.

(Photo courtesy of Michael A. Dirr, Ph.D.)

The February/Forsythia
MYSTIQUE

Intelligent
Independent
Friendly

Even before William Forsyth's time and continuing today, the Forsythia's graceful branches reflect the independent nature of the February-born individual. The unrestrained and expressive beauty of the flower mirrors their autonomy and self-direction. These are strong marks of the shrewd and clever side of those born when the Forsythia blooms.

In addition, February people are friendly and affectionate, qualities that are strongly depicted in the free-flowing appearance of the Forsythia. Its brilliant yellow blossoms also portray well the warmth of these amiable autonomous individuals.

Watching the Forsythia begin to bloom after the cold winter serves as a reminder of your innate intelligence and encourages you to develop a strong sense of independence. Forcing the lovely blooms inside (which is a little different than Narcissus forcing; see Glossary) and watching them grow will provide an intimate experience with the plant. This inside forcing requires only two things to prosper: sun and water. Its friendly, inviting appearance on the landscape will be a welcome addition not only to your garden, but also to the gardens of those to whom you care to extend the blessings of this gift.

Culture

Zone 4

pH 7

Sun/Part shade

Height: Up to 8 feet

The Olive family (Oleaceae) has about 29 genera including Forsythia, Jasminum, Ligustrum, and Osmanthus. The six or seven Forsythia species (common name Golden Bells) are among the earliest shrubs to bloom. To get February bloom where snow is on the ground, simply cut some of the long canes and place them inside a water-filled vase near a sunny window and enjoy.

Gardening
TIPS

Growing

- Early Forsythia needs full sun and loose rich soil for maximum flowering. This is a large shrub when mature, so give it plenty of room.
- Fertilize with any garden fertilizer.
- There are no insect or disease problems on healthy plants.

(Photo courtesy of Michael A. Dirr, Ph.D.)

Pruning
- Prune after blooming, but don't shear indiscriminately because you will eliminate next year's flowers and destroy the beautiful free form of the plant. Don't try to "shape" the plant.
- Cut back long stems to encourage fuller branching and flower production once every three years. To do this, reach inside the plant immediately after flowers fade and remove older branches to the ground. Since there is no real "trunk," but rather several large branches, this plant can be divided.

Propagation
- Propagate with cuttings of this year's growth in summer, or ripe wood in autumn and winter.
- This plant roots (see Glossary) easily, and does especially well if treated with root hormone.

Availability

OF FEBRUARY BIRTHFLOWER OF THE LANDSCAPE™

Forsythia blooms well outside in the lower South beginning in February; progressively later in the season the farther north you go. A wonderful characteristic of Forsythia is that regardless of the weather conditions outside, you can cut a branch and nurture it by forcing it inside (see Glossary) and be rewarded with an abundant flowering for your birthday. This way you have the double gift of inside blooms in winter and outside blooms a little while later.

In mid-May we begin to ship 8-inch pots of Lynwood Gold Forsythia to all states except California, Washington, Oregon, and New Mexico (due to soil restriction laws in these states). Individually wrapped plants and bare-root plants are also sometimes available according to the season. We must wait until after the first frost after the leaves have dropped and the plant is dormant before we can dig and ship these lovely flowers bare root. Otherwise they may wither and die. Liners (see Glossary) have a longer season of availability because they contain some soil medium that has been moistened. See Order form for pricing.

If you are interested in more information about FORSYTHIA, *contact:*

American Horticultural Society
7931 E. Boulevard Drive
Alexandria, VA 22308-1300
(703) 768-5700 or (800) 777-7931

(Photo courtesy of Michael A. Dirr, Ph.D.)

❧·AZALEA·❧
March Birthflower of the Landscape™

Flowers are lovely; love is flower-like. . .
SAMUEL TAYLOR COLERIDGE

THE FIRST WRITTEN MEMOIR of Azaleas is found in a Japanese book of poems dated 759 A.D. Even before this, exotic rhododendron (Azalea is the common name for Rhododendron) has held an imaginative place in Japanese gardens and lore. Having an inborn need for a considerable amount of atmospheric moisture, these plants have thrived for centuries between 2,000 feet and 18,000 feet above sea level in the world's highest mountains, the awesome Himalayas in northern India.

In an unwavering drive to find the most beautiful plants, and risking fortune, family, and even life itself, the imaginative explorer Frank Kingdon-Ward crisscrossed these forbidding regions on the backs of elephants in the 1920s and 1930s. Huge leeches living overhead in the humid canopy of dark rhododendron forests dropped indiscriminately on all intruders so that the native guides sometimes refused to enter these woods. This fanciful adventurer related how his bearers found a wild bees' nest and, in an attempt to enliven their monotonous diet, partook freely of the

(Photo courtesy of Fred C. Galle.)

fresh honey, which is in fact poisonous. Soon they were rendered intoxicated and practically unconscious for several days.

Kingdon-Ward's journeys were rewarded with the sighting of a 55-foot-high specimen rhododendron with a six-foot diameter trunk that bore more than 800 trusses of glistening scarlet flowers the size of soccer balls. It is through his efforts, spurred on by his intellect and emotion regarding these plants, as well as efforts of like-minded souls, that we can nonchalantly take for granted the outstanding varieties of Azalea that we find so readily available on the market today. This natural, instinctive drive to find something better is indicative of those March-born individuals associated with the Azalea.

The March/Azalea MYSTIQUE

Intuitive Creative Compassionate

The traits of those born in March certainly should be nurtured and encouraged. They are all worthy characteristics that speak of persons who possess inner direction. Those born when the Azalea blooms have a rare intuitive capacity that enables them to be compassionate and understanding of others, be they friends or strangers. As it grows and flowers so profusely every spring, the Azalea speaks to the inborn sensitivity, the natural bent toward feeling, that these individuals possess.

These instinctive traits encourage their creative side, a well of artistic talent that enriches the lives of those in contact with these March-born people. The wide variety of Azaleas encourages the expression of imaginative and ingenious ideas in those born in the third month. Planting Azaleas in your yard will add beauty and profuse color to your landscape every year. These plants are a natural indication of intuition and creativity. They will become a symbol of your kind-hearted nature to those to whom you give this lush plant. Keep the fanciful side of yourself alive by enjoying and sharing the lovely Azalea.

Opposite: *Koromo Kishibu.* **Right:** *Azalea Garden. (Photos courtesy of Fred C. Galle.)*

Culture

Zone 2

pH 6

Part Shade

Height:
2 feet to 6 feet

The Heath Family (Ericaceae) has about 70 genera, including Andromeda, Leucothoe, Pieris, Rhododendron, and Vaccinium (blueberry). The perhaps 800 Azalea or Rhododendron species (there are no consistent botanical differences between the two) are native to the temperate areas of the northern hemisphere and abundant in the Himalayas, but are not found in Africa or South America. There are thousands of species and hybrids of this delightfully perfumed plant, and many people distinguish Azaleas as generally having smaller, thinner, and deciduous leaves, while Rhododendrons generally have broad, leathery, and evergreen leaves. Most are spring bloomers, but there are several that flower in summer as well as a few in autumn. The flowers of the Azaleas are funnel-shaped, and Rhododendron flowers are usually larger and bell-shaped.

Several popular Azalea species include:

- Kurume hybrid Azaleas are slow-growing shrubs 6 to 10 feet high with small glossy evergreen leaves. Coral Bells, a cultivar of kurume species, are bicolor pink. Hino Crimson are bright red, Snow are white, and Hinodegiri are rose-red in early spring.

- Southern indica hybrid Azaleas are vigorous shrubs 8 to 10 feet high and wide with evergreen leaves and large flowers, developed in South Carolina about 1890. Favorite cultivars of the southern indica species include: Formosa (purple), George Tabor (lavender-pink), Mrs. G. G. Gerbing (white), and Pride of Mobile (vivid pink). All bloom in mid-spring in the lower South.

- Austrinum, commonly called the Florida flame Azalea, is native to the Southeast, and is hardy and easy to grow. This vigorous deciduous shrub grows 6 to 12 feet high with fragrant yellow or gold flowers in the spring.

Right: *Ben Morrison.*
Opposite: *Homebash*
Ex. *(Photos courtesy of Fred C. Galle.)*

Gardening TIPS

Growing
- These are acid-loving plants with shallow roots that need more air than many plants. To prevent root rot, plant Azalea on a mound of soil so roots can access air from all sides. Planting too deep is a common mistake of amateur gardeners.
- Azaleas like rich, humus-filled, well-drained soil and plenty of mulch.
- They will survive in full sun, but need protection from winter winds and are best planted in light shade.
- Only a few are good choices for extremely cold or hot climates.
- Scale, lacebug, and spider mites are pest problems and can be dealt with by using insecticide sprays.

Pruning
- Pruning is not obligatory, but if necessary, prune immediately after flowering.
- To increase density, remove oldest stems every three years.
- Azaleas with small leaves do not survive severe pruning well, but large-leaved Azaleas do.

Propagation
- Sow seeds in pans of sandy peat and cover slightly with sphagnum.
- Take cuttings of half-ripe wood, treat with growth hormone, and plant cuttings in a well-drained mixture of perlite and peat moss.
- Since rooting (see Glossary) is a little harder with Azaleas than with Forsythia, be sure to scratch the bark well and apply growth hormone to ensure successful rooting.

Availability

OF MARCH BIRTHFLOWER OF THE LANDSCAPE™

While much of the South is literally covered with the prolific beautiful blooms of Azaleas during March, the plant blooms later in the North due to freezes and frost. In order to have early blooms in areas that are colder, get potted Azaleas in bloom from florists in March or grow them in a greenhouse.

Commercial shipping of Azaleas (Girard's Fuschia is a variety that does well) begins in mid-May in 8-inch pots, but laws do not allow shipping of soil to California, Oregon, Washington, or New Mexico. We also ship bare root and liners (see Glossary) of Azaleas when they are available and when it is safe to do so. See order form for pricing and shipping dates.

To learn more about
AZALEAS, contact:

American Rhododendron Society
11 Pinecrest Drive
Fortuna, CA 95540
707-725-3043

Above: *Tom Everett.*
Right: *Orange Flamium.*
(*Photos courtesy of Fred C. Galle.*)

❖IRIS❖
April Birthflower
of the Landscape™

*Is there such a thing as an ugly Iris? Less pretty ones there
may be, but uglies—perish the thought! There are irises
for every soil and situation too—Spanish Irises and
English for sunny borders, and German Irises for every-
where, even London, and Ochroleuca Irises for the bog,
Cristata Irises for the rock bed and—Oncocyclus Irises for
the Kingdom of Heaven!*

REGINALD FARRER

THE IRIS HAS BEEN TRACED back as
far as 2000 B.C., during the Minoan period, on the Greek island of Crete, where
stylized artwork depicting it has been
found. The Iris has been symbolic since
the times of the ancient Greeks and
Egyptians, for whom it represented the
gods and regality, respectively, and was a
strong emblem in the Middle Ages, when
it represented chivalry. In fact, a popular
design element today—the fleur-de-lis,
Flower of Kings—originated in the
twelfth century when King of the Franks,
Clovis I, adopted the Iris as his emblem
when he embraced Christianity. Legend
has it that Clovis's army,
retreating from the Goths
and about to cross the
Rhine, saw Irises growing

Feature Attraction.

(Photo courtesy of

David Schreiner of

Schreiner's Gardens.)

far out into the water. Deciding that the water was shallow in that direction, they were able to ford the river successfully.

The strong character of this flower has captured the imagination of painters for centuries, having been depicted often by lauded artists such as the Dutch and Italian Masters, and in the twentieth century, Van Gogh and Monet. Because of the wide range of diverse and exciting colors found in the blooms, the genus was named for the rainbow goddess, Iris. The broad range of artistic uses of this dynamic and popular flower include its frequent portrayal in embroidery, paintings, cloisonné, lacquer, and carved crystal in both oriental and Persian art.

In addition to its prolific presence in the arts, the physical attributes of the Iris are used enthusiastically in cooking and commerce. The tubers are a favorite food in the Mediterranean, and the seeds are used in Alaska and Europe to concoct a robust coffee. Its rhizomes, the bulbous roots, have been hung in barrels of stouthearted beer or wine to keep the contents fresh. Several Old World species are used in perfumery, and some yield medicinal products. Besides being an inspiration to artisans, the flower's petals can be crushed into a lively pigment for paint.

The April/Iris MYSTIQUE

Energetic Assertive Courageous

The April born possess very strong characteristics that are reflected in the Iris. These people are energetic and lead active, vigorous lives. These assertive traits are evident in their positive and self-confident manner. April individuals tend to be courageous as well as strong willed.

Even though its appearance seems delicate, the Iris is as spirited and lively as those who are born when it blooms. It holds itself up confidently on strong stems as it moves animatedly in rhythm with the warming April breezes. The showers of April cannot daunt the self-assurance of this lovely blossom.

April traits are certainly worth encouraging in yourself and in those about whom you care. Pass on the fearless love of life that is exhibited enthusiastically by those born in this month, and show others they are capable of developing into strong dynamic people, too. A gift of Iris can be an impetus toward a more fulfilling, robust life. Don't hesitate to share it.

McKay iris. (Photo courtesy of David Schreiner of Schreiner's Gardens.)

Culture

Zone 4

pH 7

Sun/Part Shade

The Iris family (Iridaceae) has about 60 genera, including Crocus, Freesia, Gladiolus, and Iris. The 200 or more Iris species are native mostly to the North Temperate Zone, South Africa, and are abundant in Asia. They come in a rainbow of colors from the palest yellow to deep rich midnight black, though true reds are unknown. While each bloom does not last a long time, the plant provides a succession of vibrant blooms over a long period.

Height:
4 inches to 3 feet

A few popular species of this fascinating plant are:

- Germanica, bearded Iris, is a huge group of hybrid cultivars with flower stalks 8 inches to 3 feet high in a wide range of colors. They are easy to grow in a well-drained, humus-rich soil.
- Kaempferi, Japanese Iris, provides very large flowers up to 8 inches wide in rich shades of blue, purple, red-violet, or white. They need a lime-free soil that is constantly moist.
- Louisiana hybrids have flowers up to 7 inches wide in shades of blue, purple, pink, copper, and yellow. They tolerate hot, humid summers and prefer, but do not require, moist soil.

Gardening TIPS

Growing
- Though most Irises need sunlight and humus-rich, well-drained garden soil, a few—like the Japanese Iris and the water flag—delight in a wet spot. If your soil is acidic, add lime.
- To achieve the biggest bloom and avoid rot, leave the tops of the rhizomes (see Glossary) uncovered so that the sunlight can reach them.
- Point the fan of leaves in the direction you wish the plants to grow.
- Fertilize often with bonemeal.

Pruning
- Immediately after flowers have shriveled, pick off the dead heads and cut spent stems so all the energy of the plant can focus on strengthening other parts of the plant rather than making seed. This also improves the appearance of your garden considerably.

Propagation
- In the fall, or immediately after flowering, divide the rhizomes by cutting them into sections, making sure each section has a fan of leaves. Doing this will improve the quality of the plants that remain and give you plenty of new plants for another spot. Divide clumps of Irises every 3 to 4 years.
- You can divide this plant any time of the year. If you divide and replant Irises in August, you will have blooms the next spring. If you wait until fall, your plant will

Silvarado. (Photo courtesy of David Schreiner of Schreiner's Gardens.)

have a better chance of survival, but you'll probably have to wait another year for the plant to bloom.

- You can also propagate by seeds.

Availability
OF APRIL BIRTHFLOWER OF THE LANDSCAPE™

Dwarf Iris are usually early, blooming in April. Intermediate Iris bloom in May. (See Zone Map, page 22.) The beautiful tall varieties usually bloom in June, which is the peak season. With careful selection, it is possible to have this flower genus in bloom every month of the year. Autumn is the best time to dig these plants, though it can be done almost any time.

Commercially, we offer bare-root stock in two seasons: the spring, beginning on February 1 with stock usually sold out by March 15, and the fall, beginning on August 1, with stock selling quickly. The stock of some of the slower moving varieties sometimes lasts until around October 15. For the retailer, refrigeration might extend this commercial availability a month or so in each season; planting them in containers will extend availability even longer. To ensure availability of the flowers you want, place your orders a month or two in advance of planting time. See order form for pricing.

*To meet other people
with an interest in*
IRISES, *contact:*

American Iris Society
8426 Vine Valley Rd.
Sun Valley, CA 91352
(818) 767-5512

Opposite: *Victoria Falls iris.* (*Photo courtesy of David Schreiner of Schreiner's Gardens.*) **Above:** *Blue Diamond iris.* (*Photo courtesy of Michael A. Dirr, Ph.D.*)

❧ROSE❧

May Birthflower of the Landscape™

Go, lovely rose!
Tell her that wastes her time and me
That now she knows,
When I resemble her to thee,
How sweet and fair she seems to be.

EDMUND WALLER

THE ROSE HAS BEEN AROUND for more than thirty million years. Fossilized remains that were discovered by anthropologists have been directly connected to present-day Rose species. The first people to cultivate this plant were the Chinese, who grew it for more than 2,000 years before Europe had its first introduction to Chinese Roses in the mid-eighteenth century. Almost every American modern Rose can literally trace its roots to one of those Roses imported from China.

The heart of European Rose cultivation, however, began in Persia and Mesopotamia, where a flourishing trade of perfume grew out of the fragrant oil, attar, that was distilled from the Rose petal. The ancient Romans and Greeks each

Paradise.

(Photo courtesy of Pete Haring.)

Don Juan single.
(Photo courtesy of
Michael A. Dirr, Ph.D)

had their own thriving Rose industry as well, producing immense gardens, medicine, perfumes, decoration, and religious garlands and ornamentation.

The depiction of the Rose goes back to the oldest known picture of true Roses, the sixteenth-century B.C. House of Frescoes at Knossos, on the Greek island of Crete. The island of Rhodes in Greece (whose name itself is from "Rose") portrayed flowering Roses on its coins in 4000 B.C. And the Rose has had a prominent place in literature, having been mentioned by writers from Confucius to Horace to Shakespeare to contemporary scribes.

Interestingly, the Hildesheim Cathedral in Germany houses the oldest known living Rose tree, said to be more than 1,000 years old. In the massive destruction of life and property during WWII, Hildesheim was bombed. Miraculously, the steadfast old tree survived, although all of its top growth was decimated.

One of the world's most valuable oils, attar of Roses, is valued as the base of most perfumes. Bulgaria is the main center of production of this precious liquid and makes three quarters of the world's supply. More than 200,000 workers tend the bushes, gather the petals, and distill the oil. A ton of petals yields a mere pound of active attar, most of which is shipped to France to be further refined.

The May/Rose MYSTIQUE

Dependable Productive Practical

Roses are the centuries-old symbol of steadfastness possessed by dependable May-born individuals. The unfailing beauty of the Rose suggests the faithfulness often found among these people. As the Rose in the garden blooms, it becomes an emblem of the productive and dynamic side of those who claim it as a Birthflower.

The practical side of those born under the fragrance of the Rose shows in their understanding of this flower as a solid and indispensable foundation plant for any garden. It, more than any other flower, speaks to us as it has to innumerable poets and artists throughout the centuries.

The Rose responds to those who give it care by blooming faithfully. In turn, the level of care given to the Rose is indicative of our capacity to care for others. It is therefore a symbol of our loyalty when it is presented as a token of friendship. People born in May have the special, unfailing ability to pass on these traits of productivity and dependability to anyone who will accept and cherish the gift of a Rose. To discover the truth in this you merely have to try it.

Culture

Zone 4

pH 6.5

Sun/Part Shade

Height:
4 inches to 10 feet

The Rose family (Rosaceae) has about 100 genera, including Cotoneaster, Fragaria (strawberry), Photinia, Prunus (peaches, plums, almonds, cherries), Pyracantha, Rosa (Rose), and Spiraea. The more than 100 Rose species have been modified through selection and hybridization, thus giving rise to some 20,000 cultivars, including many of the most fragrant plants and ornamentals in the North Temperate Zone.

Some of the most popular contemporary Rose classes include:

- Hybrid teas, usually sold in the form of grafted plants (see Glossary), are considered the epitome of the perfect Rose. Though attention should be paid to the insect and disease problems that face this particular plant, loving care will bring rich rewards. They generally bear one flower per stem and are the "long-stemmed Roses" of the florist industry.
- Floribundas, which result from the cross between hybrid teas and polyanthas, are best purchased in the form of grafted plants. Constant season-long, medium-size blooms in clusters in a full range of colors are characteristic. European is red, Iceberg is white, Sexy Rexy is pink, and Sunsprite is yellow.
- Grandifloras, the result of crosses between floribundas and hybrid teas, combine vigor and blooming ability with beautiful blooms and long stems. This results in plants generally hardier than hybrid teas, but which still require full winter protection. They, too, are best purchased as grafted plants.
- Miniature Roses are characterized by a combination of ever-blooming small flowers on thin stems and tiny foliage that remains or can be maintained at less than 18 inches in height. Probably the hardiest of the bush Roses, many survive temperatures below zero degrees Fahrenheit.
- Climbing Roses are best purchased as grafted plants where winters are mild, since protecting them from the winter is quite troublesome. Reaching heights of 10 feet or more, they range in flower form from large-flowered to small-clustered in a full range of colors.
- Shrub Roses are commonly fully winter hardy and are grown for both their flowers and their hips (see Glossary), which attract birds during the winter.
- Old-fashioned species Roses are valued for their simple beauty and ease of care that allows them to thrive where no other Roses will grow. Often fragrant with colorful hips, most are shrub Roses, though some are climbers. They offer excellent resistance to pests and disease. They are the only Roses that come true from seed and can be propagated by division or cuttings.

Sunsprite.

(Photo courtesy of Pete Haring.)

Gardening TIPS

Growing
- Winter hardiness is extremely variable in Roses.
- Space the plants depending on the eventual, full-grown size of the variety chosen.
- They will do best in open, sunny locations with humus-rich, well-drained soil that is not near invading tree roots. Replace mulch with new mulch in winter to remove potential insect and disease problems.
- Spray regularly for insects and diseases. Not all Roses have these problems, so you should become familiar with the needs of your chosen plants.
- Fertilize according to the need of your particular Rose plant.

Pruning
- Remove faded flowers to ensure continued bloom except on shrub Roses, which will produce their attractive fruit (hips).
- Remove branches killed in winter and older stems in the spring by cutting the stems at 6 inches above ground level.

Propagation
- Taking rooted cuttings (see Glossary) is the most practical method of propagation for the gardener.

Availability
OF MAY BIRTHFLOWER OF THE LANDSCAPE™

Frost prevents any Roses from blooming outside in northern areas in May. (See Zone Map, page 22.) Insect and disease problems discourage many hybrid tea Rose growers, but many of the hardy old garden varieties can put the joy back into the hearts of all Rose lovers. Our commercial bare-root shipping usually runs December 12 to March 12, with the best choices running out of stock early.

Our first choices to ship to you are varieties that have excellent disease resistance and offer ease in growing. Place your order early to ensure delivery of your choice of the world's most popular flower. See order form for pricing.

For more information on ROSES, *contact:*

American Rose Society
P.O. Box 30000
Shreveport, LA 71130
(318) 938-5402

Opposite: *Sweet Vivien.* *(Photo courtesy of Pete Haring.)* **Above:** *(Photo courtesy of Michael A. Dirr, Ph.D.)*

❧HYDRANGEA❧

June Birthflower of the Landscape™

*Show me your garden, provided it be your own,
and I will tell you what you are like.*

ALFRED AUSTIN

DUE TO JAPAN'S ISOLATIONISM in the sixteenth, seventeenth, and eighteenth centuries, the Hydrangea, while a popular garden flower in Japan, was not shared with the rest of the world. The Hydrangea did not make an appearance in the Western world until the early 1700s, when in 1739 Sir Joseph Banks introduced in Britain the Hydrangea Maritima, a specimen from a Chinese garden. At the same time, the name Hydrangea—from the Greek words *hydro* (water) and *angeion* (vase)—began to appear in Western botanical literature: The first use was by Jan Frederik Gronovius, a Swedish botanist who established the binomial nomenclature system, to describe the plant in his *Flora Virginica* in 1739. The more famous Carolus Linnaeus also named the same plant in his *Species Planetarium* in 1753. The Hydrangea flourished as an ornamental plant in gardens throughout Europe and England.

Because the Hydrangea is very responsive to soil composition and sensitive to the amount of aluminum it absorbs, the environment of the plant itself determines whether its blooms are pink or blue. However, there are some white-blooming Hydrangeas that will produce

Penny Mac.

(Photo courtesy of

Penny McHenry.)

only white flowers. In addition, a shortage of iron in the soil can cause the plant's leaves to become yellow, with green near the veins. Also, the leaves will usually show a sensitivity to dry conditions by wilting and drooping.

Versatile and expressive, the Hydrangea grows in many forms, depending on the species. Some grow to be trees as high as 25 feet. Others grow as vines that run horizontally over the ground, making a shade-loving ground cover.

The June/Hydrangea MYSTIQUE

**Responsive
Communicative
Versatile**

Anyone with a birthday timed when the Hydrangea blooms can rejoice in the possession of traits that contribute to their expansive nature. They tend to be very responsive to their surroundings as well as to the people in their lives. These versatile individuals are accomplished in a variety of ways and are often gifted with abilities in a number of areas. Free-spoken and communicative, they are very open and friendly toward others in general.

The multi-faceted nature of those born in June is mirrored in the Hydrangea, which, because of its sensitivity to its environment, can express beauty in an array of wonderful ways. The lushness of the leaves, as well as the rich hues of its blooms, is reflective of multi-talented people born when Hydrangeas burst with color. The clusters of flowers grow so closely together that they appear to be one giant, gorgeous bloom. June individuals respond to others in the same way; because of their ability to be receptive to the needs of people around them, their special talents are often expressed in their relationships with others. What better way to communicate to someone that you care about their feelings, hopes, and dreams than to give them a gift that so aptly expresses your responsive nature?

Left: *Nikko Blue.* *(Photo courtesy of Michael A. Dirr, Ph.D.)* **Opposite: *Penny Mac.*** *(Photo courtesy of Penny McHenry.)*

Culture

Zone 4

pH 7

Part Shade

Height:
4 feet to 10 feet
for shrubs

The Saxifrage family (Saxifragaceae) has about 80 genera, including Astilbe, Hydrangea, Ribes, and Saxifraga. The 23 Hydrangea species of erect or climbing, deciduous or evergreen shrubs are native to North America and South America and East Asia.

A few of these especially popular and beautiful species are:

- Macrophylla, an evergreen shrub found in mild climates, grows to 8 feet and produces very large blue, pink, or white flowers up to Zone 6 (see Zone Map, page 22). Some of these plants will produce blue flowers if grown in acidic soil or soil sprinkled with sulfur. The acid in the soil enhances the absorption of aluminum which promotes the blue blooms. The depth of color deepens as more aluminum is absorbed. Conversely the flowers will be pink if the plant is grown in alkaline soil or soil sprinkled with lime.

- Paniculata, a shrub or small tree, grows to as high as 30 feet and produces large, showy, long-lasting flowers of white (which age to a pink color) up to Zone 4 (see Zone Map, page 22).

- Quercifolia, an oakleaf Hydrangea (its leaves resemble the leaves of oak trees), grows to 6 feet high, up to Zone 5 (see Zone Map, page 22). A North American native, this plant produces showy clusters of large white flowers in May and June, which can turn to pink or tan later in the summer. Its coarse-textured leaves often turn a rich, reddish-purple in autumn.

Possibly the most flamboyant of all large shrubs, a main attraction of the Hydrangea is its long-lasting flowers that can be harvested for beautiful, longer-lasting dried arrangements.

Opposite: *Lilacina.*
Right: *Snowflake.*
(Photos courtesy of Penny McHenry.)

Gardening TIPS

Growing
- Give this plant plenty of room for its eventual mature size.
- Hydrangeas require humus-rich, somewhat moist, porous soil. Mulch them well and water during dry periods.
- They bloom most profusely in full sun, but have a higher survival rate in partial shade.
- Powdery mildew may be a pest problem.

Pruning
- Dead-heading helps stimulate blooms for the next year and helps prevent winter snow damage caused by weight added to the already heavy, dry flower clusters.
- Removing old canes or severely pruning every few years in early spring can improve the growth pattern, making the shrub fuller and growth less erratic.
- Some can be pruned to a tree form.

Propagation
- Propagate hardy species in summer by taking 4- to 6-inch green cuttings (new growth that hasn't turned brown). Remove any leaves from the bottom of the cutting and dip that end of the cutting into a root hormone, available at garden centers. Plant 2 inches deep in moist, sandy soil in a box. Cover the box with glass to maintain humidity and stimulate growth and rooting.

Availability
OF JUNE BIRTHFLOWER OF THE LANDSCAPE™

Hydrangea macrophylla Nikko Blue has impressive large blue or pink flowers that bloom throughout summer and into early autumn. We selected this particular plant for its fantastic flowers. We ship beginning in May in 8-inch pots to all states except California, Oregon, Washington, and New Mexico due to legal soil restrictions (see Chapter II). Bare root and liners also are available to all states. See order form for pricing.

To learn more about
HYDRANGEAS,
contact:

American Hydrangea Society
P.O. Box 11645
Atlanta, GA 30355
(404) 636-7886

Above: *Ayesha.* *(Photo courtesy of Penny McHenry.)* **Right:** *Nikko Blue.* *(Photo courtesy of Michael A. Dirr, Ph.D.)*

CRAPE MYRTLE

July Birthflower of the Landscape™

And where a little terrace from its bowers
Of blooming myrtle . . .
Scatters its sense-dissolving fragrance o'er
The liquid marble of the windless lake.

PERCY BYSSHE SHELLEY

THE MOST COMMON ASSOCIATION people have with the Crape Myrtle is as an old-fashioned plant found in the elegant gardens of the Deep South. But in the last thirty years, the emergence of a New South, with its prominent artistic, social, and civic presence, has had as its companion the clever transformation of the common Crape Myrtle into a popular and versatile plant in contemporary gardens and lawns. These improvements have taken shape in the unusual and inventive breeding and selecting of new cultivars, which have expanded the size and colors of the wonderful Crape Myrtle.

More than fifty years ago the first of these unusual Crape Myrtles were introduced from Asia to southern American landscapes, where responsive Southern gardeners quickly recognized the plant's constant ornamental qualities. But it was due to the imaginative and clever efforts of Dr. Donald R. Egolf of the U.S. National Arboretum in Washington, D.C., that hybrid cultivars of Crape Myrtle that were resistant to mildew were developed. He Americanized them further by loyally naming those cultivars after Native American tribes.

Hopi. (Photo courtesy of Michael A. Dirr, Ph.D.)

Inventive growers and breeders have developed a wide range of cultivars, from dwarf Crape Myrtles that rise just a few inches above the ground (excellent when used as a ground cover in sunny spots) to small trees that can shoot up to more than twenty feet high. Dwarf cultivars of Crape Myrtle are the earliest blooming, some beginning as early as late spring, and some of the taller varieties continue blooming into late fall. With the right mix of cultivars, you can have this loyal tree/shrub dotting your property with color for the better part of a year.

The July/Crape Myrtle
MYSTIQUE

Sensitive Imaginative Loyal

Being born in the month of July marks a person as a sensitive, feeling individual. This perceptive nature extends into the realm of the creative and imaginative. One who has a July birthday is sure to be a loyal friend or companion who can be counted on to be devoted to those who are important in his or her life.

This same steadfastness is apparent in the Crape Myrtle as it brings beauty regularly to us throughout all the seasons of the year. Even without its lovely blossoms and tender leaves, it shows us its impressive, striking bark in the winter. In the fall the leaves burn with intense reds and yellows, revealing the plant's sensitive and imaginative side.

Be responsive to the creative side of yourself and plant one or more of these truly wonderful trees. They will grace your landscape with the anticipation and promise of intense color for months before the blossoms come alive. After the brighter colors of the flowers are gone, the rich hues of its fall foliage take over, and finally the softer tones of its satiny bark will give you a sense of its constant, comforting presence during the winter months.

What better symbol of a true and faithful friend can there be than the gift of a Crape Myrtle? Those to whom you send this plant will never fail to think of you and your dependability and sensitivity as they see the grace of the tree. Take advantage of the opportunity to be present with those important people in a very special way throughout the years.

Byers Wonderful White.

(Photo courtesy of David Byers.)

Culture

Zone 7

pH 6.5

Sun

Height:
3 feet to 25 feet

The Loosestrife family (Lythraceae) has about 22 genera, including Lagerstroemia (common name, Crape Myrtle), whose 55 species are native to the warmer parts of Asia and the Pacific islands. Characteristic of the ornamental Crape Myrtle is a small tree that is multi-stemmed with smooth, beautiful bark that peels off, adding attractive interest to its countenance in the wintertime. In northern areas they are sometimes grown in the greenhouse as pot plants, or in the ground as annuals.

Gardening TIPS

Growing
- A summer favorite because the most profuse blooms are dependable through July, the Crape Myrtle does not flower well in the shade.
- The U.S. National Arboretum has developed about 20 new cultivated varieties which are hardy to Zone 6 and exhibit better mildew resistance.
- While Crape Myrtle is easy to cultivate and thrives in most garden soils that are well drained, mulch and medium-to-high application of fertilizer keep it even happier.
- This plant is subject to powdery mildew, which can be controlled by spraying with a fungicide available at garden centers.

Pruning
- Pruning spent flowers will encourage additional bloom.
- Removing lower limbs allows the plant to assume a tree form, while pruning it to six inches from the ground in March will help the plant maintain smaller shrub size.

Propagation
- Propagate either by seeds or by cuttings under glass. For more information on this procedure, refer to the Propagation section of Chapter VI, Hydrangea.

Tusca Vare. (Photo courtesy of Michael A. Dirr, Ph.D.)

Availability

OF JULY BIRTHFLOWER OF THE LANDSCAPE™

Guaranteed hardy only in Zones 7 through Zone 9 (see Zone Map, page 22), this summer-flowering beauty is everybody's favorite. Dwarfed varieties that are heavily mulched against the cold will survive the winter a little farther north as a perennial that returns every year from its roots.

When available, we can ship liners or bare-root lagerstroemia indicia Nana (semi dwarf) or Peppermint Crape Myrtle, which is a beautiful large shrub with an attractive mottled gray main stem. Its flowers have crinkled petals which are dark pink laced with cinnamon. See pricing and order form.

We were unable to locate a Crape Myrtle club or society in the United States for hobbyists and collectors that would sponsor shows and contests, publish a magazine, and promote the plant in general.

To learn more about
CRAPE MYRTLE, *you might try contacting:*

Friends of the U.S. National Arboretum
3299 K Street NW, 7th Floor
Washington, DC 70007
(202) 965-7510

Opposite: *Red.*

Above: *Catawba.*

*(Photos courtesy of
David Byers.)*

CHAPTER VIII

❀ PHLOX ❀
August Birthflower of the Landscape™

It does give a sumptuous glowing show, especially if you can plant it in a half-shady bed where its colours will curiously change with the sinking sun and will deepen with twilight into colours you never thought it possessed.

VITA SACKVILLE-WEST, on Phlox

NEARLY ALL PHLOX are native to North America, with only slight representations of the colorful plant in South America, Europe, and northern Asia. Persistent British hybridists are mostly responsible for transforming these demure individuals into the splendid outstanding cultivars of today. And what a masterful job they have done! Today the Phlox is an especially popular member of both rock and border gardens—with its loose clusters of flowers in an amazing array of strong, clean colors, its long blooming season, and its steady, successful performance as a border garden flower.

Unlike the adventurous world explorers of the eighteenth century, the obstacles facing the U.S. nurserymen when exporting these graceful alluring

(Photo courtesy of Michael A. Dirr, Ph.D.)

beauties lies not in the danger of actually shipping them, but within our country's bureaucracy. Florida has been allowed to export the tender, gentle Phlox in sterile media to Europe for less than twenty years. Hawaii only received permission from the U.S. government to do this in 1994. To share the charming Phlox with the rest of the world is, at the present time, a bit challenging.

The August/Phlox
MYSTIQUE

Fair Charming Kind

But it is easy to share this Birthflower's personality traits with those you love. The Birthflower of August exemplifies the harmonious qualities of those born in this month. A truly charming flower, the Phlox highlights the enchanting qualities of the August person. With its captivating array of colors and its fetching appearance, it suggests the winsome personalities of those born when this colorful plant is opening itself for our enjoyment. Its simplicity personifies their honest and fair attributes. These kind individuals can claim the Phlox as a token of their gentle qualities.

To further develop these fine personality qualities within yourself and to keep yourself mindful of the desire to strengthen them, go to a friend's garden and ask to divide the Phlox beds so that you may transfer some to your own garden. Not only will your friend's garden be more attractive by timely thinning of plants, but you will also have a beautiful reminder of your friendship. If you cannot get Phlox from another garden, keep in constant view or on your person a picture of its charming graceful blooms that someone you hold dear has given to you. It works.

Why not also share this enchanting plant with friends and family? Having Phlox in their gardens will tend to heighten their natural bent toward developing traits of graciousness. As the blooms return each year, the tendency toward becoming a more fascinating individual will return in even stronger measure.

(Photo courtesy of Michael A. Dirr, Ph.D.)

Culture

Zone 4

pH 7

Sun/Part Shade

Height:
6 inches to 3 feet

The Phlox family (Polemoniaceae) has 18 genera, including Phlox and Polemonium (Jacob's ladder) that are native chiefly to North America. The 60 or so Phlox species of annuals or perennial herbs have many forms. They offer wonderful color, are great for cutting, and are easy to grow, all of which contribute to their extreme popularity.

Three of these species include:

- Paniculata, a sweetly scented garden Phlox, has strong stems 3 to 4 inches tall topped with large clusters of 1-inch, disc-shaped florets of white, pink, purple, red, or pale blue flowers. These bloom in the summer.
- Stolonifera is a creeping Phlox that spreads by creeping stems that root. It flowers best in partial shade and offers small purple, white, or pink flowers in spring. Blue Ridge has larger beautiful blue flowers.
- Subulata — commonly called thrift, moss pink, or creeping Phlox — is an evergreen creeper about 6 inches high and is covered with loose clusters of bright purple, pink, or white flat blossoms in early spring. For environment it prefers poor, well-drained soil and full sun with low fertilizer and moisture. After flowering, shear this species to 3 inches to encourage denser growth.

Gardening TIPS

Growing
- Any garden soil will do, but the best and longest-lasting flower is achieved in humus-rich, well-drained soil, in full sun or light shade, and provide plenty of water and fertilizer during the summer.
- Never let Phlox endure drought while the plant is actively growing.
- Watch closely for tiny red spider mites and use the appropriate insecticide if any are found.
- Powdery mildew or fungus problems are alleviated by keeping plants 18 inches apart to promote air circulation. Most Phlox Paniculata cultivars must be sprayed with a fungicide regularly during humid weather to prevent this mildew. Other species are more resistant.

Pruning
- Deadhead these plants to prolong bloom and prevent self-seeding.
- Divide every three years to keep them vigorous.

Propagation
- Divide in late fall or take strong young shoots from the root as the plant spreads in the spring.

Paniculata. (Photo courtesy of Michael A. Dirr, Ph.D.)

Availability

OF AUGUST BIRTHFLOWER OF THE LANDSCAPE™

From September 15 to December 15, you might request a white Miss Lingard, a native plant which is tall and yields beautiful, full flowers with a delicate, fresh scent. Another decided attraction is that Miss Lingard is commonly mildew resistant and has a long bloom season.

The most desirable perennial flower of all, garden Phlox bloom in profusion with huge 5- to 6-inch flower heads all summer long, June to September. The flowers are fragrant and showy on plants that grow to 2 to 3 feet tall and they make excellent cut flowers. An order from us of 48 hardy garden Phlox brings you 12 each of 4 colors — red, pink, purple, and white. See order form for pricing.

No societies of people concentrating on growing the largest or smallest, brightest or most unusual shape, or just plain the most beautiful Phlox ever, were found.

Why not start one?

Send me your name and address.

Opposite: Paniculta. (Photo courtesy of Michael A. Dirr, Ph.D.) Left: Paniculta. (Photo courtesy of Linton McKnight.)

❧·CANNA·❧

September Birthflower of the Landscape™

And God has taken a flower of gold
And broken it, and used therefrom
The mystic link to bind and hold
Spirit to matter till death come.

ROBERT FROST

ORIGINATING IN THE MARSHY AREAS of tropical and subtropical America, many Cannas have made their way across the world and have become naturalized in parts of Africa and Asia. Their fleshy roots provide a staple food to the natives of Ecuador and Colombia. In addition, some of these natives use the leaves of the plants for thatching their homes and also to wrap newborn children. Many other cultures also use the leaves to wrap food, and make use of the plant's hard black seeds in jewelry and ornamentation.

In 1846, M. Année, a gifted French diplomat at Valparaiso in Chile, brought with him to Paris a collection of Cannas from South America. Wildly successful in hybridizing the species, he deserves credit for efficiently and systematically laying the foundation for the hot and vivid

Rosemond Cole.

(Photo courtesy of Horne Canna Farm.)

colors we seem to take for granted today.

Cannas possess an abundance of attractive cultivation qualities: quick to establish, easy to maintain, low in cost. In addition, spectacular flowers and lush foliage, coupled with a long blooming season, may make the productive and efficient Canna the best buy your local garden center has to offer. They are large, effective, and impressive plants that bloom from July to the first frost and are proficiently showy during the September birth month.

The September/Canna
MYSTIQUE

Analytical Conscientious Efficient

The characteristics of those born when the brilliant colors of Canna burst to their zenith may seem, at first glance, less romantic and more rigid than those of other months, but these qualities are very meaningful and vital for these persons to strive to enhance in themselves, as well as to encourage in their circle of friends and loved ones.

A gift of the productive Canna carries the imprint of the efficient and capable September individual and encourages the recipient to foster his own capabilities. An analytical Canna-touched person can share the logical and organized features of his personality through this lovely plant. The conscientious nature of those Canna-influenced people can be nurtured in others through bestowing either the plant or a lovely gift item with the flower represented on it.

Not only can giving the Canna help to serve as a means of sharing these positive traits, but also growing it in a person's own garden or yard will intensify the systematic way in which these traits are embellished. What better way to heighten the capable, dutiful, and organized traits in yourself than to include Canna in your landscape?

Left: *Canna Garden.* *(Photo courtesy of Michael A. Dirr, Ph.D.)* **Opposite: *Richard Wallace.*** *(Photo courtesy of Horne Canna Farm.)*

Culture

Zone 7

pH 7

Sun/Part Shade

Height:
2 feet to 6 feet

The Canna Family (Cannaceae) consists of one genus native to tropical and subtropical regions, and the plants will not tolerate freezing. Of the approximately 60 Canna species, most are cultivated as hybrids of mixed parentage. Even the dwarf varieties of Canna grow large, 2 to 3 feet tall. Cultivars have broad leaves that are often colored and large clusters of very showy flowers in bright, hot colors such as blazing orange, vivid scarlet, warm yellow, but no one has ever found a blue one. These flowers look wonderful against neutral backgrounds such as walls. Blooms begin in July and continue until the first frost kills them to the ground.

Gardening
TIPS

Growing
- Cannas are easy to cultivate in any moist, fertile soil high in humus and mulched well to protect against freezing.
- These moisture- and sun-loving plants are also excellent pot or tub plants on a porch or patio. They can even be grown as water plants.
- Cannas can be attacked by an insect pest called a leaf roller, but this problem is easily controlled by applying carbaryl (Sevin), available at garden centers.
- Fertilize monthly with ordinary fertilizer (10-10-10, see Glossary).
- In the North, dig the roots (rhizomes) before the first freeze and store them in a warm dry place. Rhizomes may be started indoors one month or more before planting outside. Cannas can be left in the ground in the Deep South.

Pruning
- For more prolific bloom, remove spent flower heads by cutting or breaking just below the dead bloom, being careful not to harm the new clusters.
- In the South, after the first frost, cut foliage to 6 inches and mulch well.
- Thin plants every two to three years by digging and dividing the rhizomes.

Propagation
- Roots are easily divided by cutting into pieces, each with 2 or 3 eyes. Start a new garden area with extra rhizomes.
- Seed germination of Canna is possible, but because the seed coat is very hard, germination is difficult if you do not scratch the seed (by nicking with a knife or scratching with sandpaper) before proceeding. Revealing the seed's white interior will encourage the germination process.

Lenape. (Photo courtesy of Michael A. Dirr, Ph.D.)

Above: ***Black Knight.***

Opposite: ***Striped Beauty.***

(Photos courtesy of Horne Canna Farm.)

Availability

OF SEPTEMBER BIRTHFLOWER OF THE LANDSCAPE™

In the North (see Zone Map, page 22), Cannas should be dug and stored after the first frost. Alternatively, because they cannot withstand being frozen, they may be treated as annuals, left in the ground to die and fertilize the soil.

Shipping commercially begins February 15 and usually ends around May 1. Unless otherwise specified, we like to ship a red Canna, the President, which is a semi-dwarf that grows to three feet. However, orders may be shipped in an assortment of colors. Simply let us know what you would like on your order form.

No societies were found.
Why not start one?
Send me your name and address.

❧ DAYLILY ❧

October Birthflower of the Landscape™

All the wars of the world, all the Caesars, have not the staying power of a lily in a cottage border.
REGINALD FARRER

DAYLILIES HAVE BEEN CULTIVATED IN China for thousands of years and for many reasons other than ornamental. As a food product their blooms and buds are tasty and nutritious, and their roots and crowns are used in medicine. The juice of the root is an effective antidote for arsenic poisoning as well as an antidepressant, often referred to as a "dispeller of woe" by ancient apothecaries. The tough, dried foliage can be woven into a cord and then used for making footwear.

The 15th through 18th centuries were a great era of exploration in which vigorous and hardy men set out to map and measure the world. These expeditions included geographers, geologists, botanists, and even individual pacesetters striking out on their own with the sole intention of discovering new plants to bring back to Europe. Daylilies made their way to points

Garden Style.

(Photo courtesy of Enman R. Joiner.)

beyond China by trade routes established by such explorers. The first printed description of Daylilies appeared in 1629, and claimed that these flowers were most happy in boggy areas found in what is now Germany. The Daylily then made the journey across the Atlantic to North America with settlers leaving Europe and Great Britain.

It wasn't until 1934 when an American botanist, scholar, and plant breeder, Dr. Arlow B. Scott, published his book, *Daylilies*, that the way was paved for future breeders. It is from his hybrids that the genetic base of modern hybrids stems. And it is from his classification of the species that many botanists believe a revision of the classification of Daylily from a genera of the Lily family (Lilaceae) to a new family of its own (Hemerocallidaceae) should be made today.

The sturdy Daylily can be seen flowering in the frigid Arctic Lapland, and this spirited plant thrives in the scorching tropics as well. Daylilies are bred in Europe, the United States, New Zealand, and Australia with some cultivars being more fragile than others. Since glossy garden catalogs often do not tell you which varieties will flourish vigorously and flower abundantly in your part of the world, it is wise to visit gardens in your area to see for yourself. There you may see sprightly Daylilies that bloom from the last spring frost until the first fall freeze, and you will be able to select a hardy variety that produces lush blooms on your birthday every year.

The October/Daylily
MYSTIQUE

**Exuberant
Leader
Powerful**

The spirited Daylily is the perfect symbol of the exuberant and vigorous October individual. These lively people live abundantly full lives and are eager to share their enthusiastic lifestyle with others. Giving any of the many wonderful Daylily plants to others will add a great deal to the lives of both the giver and the recipient.

Powerful October people are natural leaders and can be thought of as pacesetters. A Daylily plant can cultivate this strong attribute, and when shared with others in whatever form chosen, can intensify the desire to become a more outgoing person, a pathfinder. The welcome sight of these flowers will embellish both landscape and spirit.

Persons whose birth was influenced by the Daylily can be described as hardy and robust. At times, these individuals may seem invincible. The sturdy Daylily is just as indomitable in spirit and symbolizes a strength that complements the leadership qualities which are the earmark of those October people.

Allow the enhancement of all these positive attributes in yourself and spread the desire to possess them to others. A gift of this luxuriant plant or an item emblazoned with this flower will be a constant reminder to the recipient of the contagious enthusiasm of the gift-giver. In turn it will spur one toward the embellishment or acquisition of the best of these traits.

(Photo courtesy of Michael A. Dirr, Ph.D.)

Culture

Zone 4

pH 6.5-7

Sun/Part Shade

Height:
1 to 3 feet

The Lily family (Lilaceae) has about 240 genera, including Asparagus, Hemerocallis, Hosta, Hyacinthus, Lilium, Liriope, Scilla, Smilax, Trillium, and Tulipa. (Much confusion is caused by some plants currently classified as Lilies that, to be botanically correct, should be reclassified since they belong to other families of plants.) The 15 or so Hemerocallis (common name Daylily) species are native from Europe to China and Japan.

Extensively hybridized and improved in recent years, Daylilies have more than 30,000 cultivars, with the original species being less commonly planted. Each individual blossom opens, matures, and withers within 24 hours or less, but as many as 30 to 50 flowers may be on a stem. Blooms from May through October can be accomplished by varying the selection of cultivars. May through July are the months of heaviest bloom in most areas for this delightfully rewarding and exuberant bloomer. October bloom can be best accomplished by proper fertilizer and watering of rebloomers as outlined in the next section.

Gardening TIPS

Growing

- Easy to grow in any good, humus-rich, well-drained garden soil in full sun, Daylilies benefit from partial shade in the South. Mulching helps keep weeds out and keeps the garden looking nicer.
- These plants are virtually carefree and have very few disease or pest problems.
- The dwarf varieties are wonderful additions to rock gardens.
- Daylilies may be dug and transplanted with little difficulty at any time of the year.
- Fertilize in May using an all-purpose granular garden fertilizer. To increase the probability of re-blossoming, continue fertilizing every two to three weeks with a liquid fertilizer. Although more expensive, some of the newer slow-release fertilizers offer an option for consistent, continuous fertilization throughout the season. Advantages of this type of fertilizer include time- and labor-saving one-time application and the fact that they do not burn plants. Water when dry.

Pruning

- Deadhead (see Glossary, page 121) flowers when bloom is over. Deadheading is not as essential for Daylilies as it is for other flowers, but removing seed pods early will encourage foliage growth.
- After all the blooms are spent, remove stems to improve garden appearance.

Propagation

- Dig and separate plants every three years, in the fall (for best survival rate) or spring (easiest time to separate), to yield more plants and improve the visual appeal of those replanted in the same spot. Share your extra plants or re-plant them in a new area.

Rebecca Marie.
(Photo courtesy of
Enman R. Joiner.)

Availability
OF OCTOBER BIRTHFLOWER OF THE LANDSCAPE™

 Daylily is a wonderful, hardy, and very easy-to-grow perennial. Flowers appear in early, mid-season, and late varieties, providing blossoms from May through October (six months) in a vast array of colors, with the exception of blue and true white. As with most perennials, each variety flowers for an average of only about two weeks. Planting several varieties can provide continuous bloom throughout the season. (In the North they like full sun, while in the South, they prefer partial shade.) The best October flowering variety is Stella d'Oro, which normally will bloom profusely right up to the first frost. It also does well in container gardens.

Commercial shipping usually begins February 1, ending March 1, with rarely anything but the slower-selling varieties left. To avoid missing desired varieties, order early. Our favorite way to ship is an assorted package of 48, including 8 each of 6 varieties and colors, ranging in bloom from early through mid season to late season. Each can be shipped individually wrapped with peat moss and ready for planting. However, our goal is to satisfy your preferences, so simply indicate them on the order form.

Hobbyists and others interested in growing DAYLILIES *for fun should contact:*

American Hemerocallis Society
P. O. Box 10
Dexter, Georgia 31019
912-875-4110

Opposite: **Garden view of Daylilies.**
Above: **Baby Fresh.** *(Photos courtesy of*
Enman R. Joiner.)

❧·CHRYSANTHEMUM·❧
November Birthflower of the Landscape™

*The white chrysanthemum
Even when lifted to the eye
Remains immaculate.*

KYORIASKO HYOKAI

THE CHRYSANTHEMUM—commonly called mum—was first introduced into Britain in the 1790s, where hybridists increased the size, varied the shape, and enhanced the color range to produce the magnificent mums we have today. Deriving its name from the Greek words *chryos* (gold) and *anthos* (flower), the Chrysanthemum is one of the world's most popular, intriguing, and adaptable plants. Its size ranges from the enormous Japanese cushion mum blooms, which can measure up to 12 inches in diameter, to the intense daisy-like potted plants capable of bearing several hundred small flowers in a single pot.

About 500 B.C. the Chinese philosopher Confucius wrote the first recorded reference to the Chrysanthemum, and for centuries the flower was cultivated in China for both medicinal purposes and its outstanding beauty. (Even today certain Chrysanthemums are used in salads in the Orient.) Records show that a Chrysanthemum Show was held in 900 A.D. in Japan and, in fact, the "rising sun" in the Japanese flag is not the sun but rather a Chrysanthemum represented by a central disc and 16 radiating petals.

In 1798, three plants were imported to France from China by M. Blanchard, an enthusiastic French merchant. The following

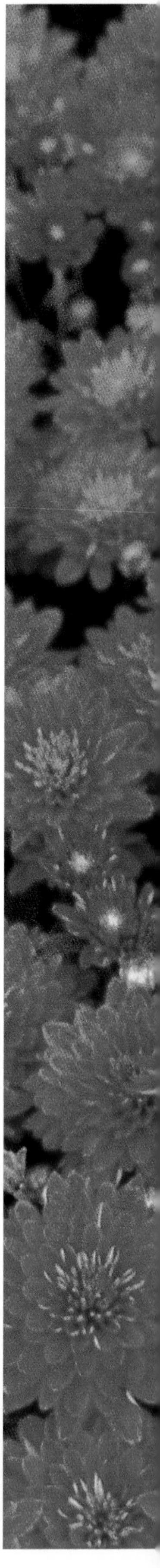

Red Remarkable.

(Photo courtesy of Yoder Brothers, Inc.)

year, plants arrived in England, leading to the first exhibition of a British seedling in December, 1832. Soon the hearts of thousands of enthusiastic amateur gardeners were captured by this versatile plant. Even today it is the amateur gardener who is taking over the breeding of new cultivars from professional nurserymen in the search for the visionary, ideal, and perfect mum.

Most of the Chrysanthemums sold by supermarkets and garden centers have been raised by professional nurserymen and are properly named, but unfortunately the clerks at these stores often are unable to give the customer any advice on the mature color, type, or eventual height of the plant. This kind of plant buying can result in the buyer unnecessarily growing plants that are inappropriate for his site or purpose.

Plants from these sources may be cheaper, but there is always the risk that they were supplied from an amateur local grower who may have stock that is not pure or true. Therefore an astute buyer, after making a selection from a catalog, will purchase Chrysanthemums from a specialized nursery. When in doubt, use two resources that are closer than you might think: a friend's garden and a local, trustworthy nursery with a good reputation. Go visit your friend's garden, and, if certain Chrysanthemums thrive in their garden, chances are these same type of plants will grow for you as well. Or call the nursery and ask for their advice on the plant you require. That way you can feel confident about your purchase and probably can find one that flowers on your birthday every year.

The November/Chrysanthemum
MYSTIQUE

Idealistic
Intense
Emotional

The Chrysanthemum has long been the symbol of a November-born person. It embodies the romantic, idealistic nature of these fervent and emotional autumn people. In many ways, the Chrysanthemum encourages the cultivation of these often visionary traits. People born when the intense colors of mums emerge are optimistic and possess an enthusiasm for life. Their focus is concentrated on getting the most out of each day they live.

The warm colors of the blossoms strike sentimental chords within us and often stir wishful and hopeful dreams in one's heart. The fervent growth of the plant year after year only increases its suggestion of a passion that belongs to November people. Place this emblem of radiant warmth within the reach of others by giving the plant itself or a symbol of the flower on a gift item to show someone that they are special to you. It may well prompt responsive behavior in that person toward a more ardent pursuit of life.

Flowers traditionally have been given as an expression of sentiment often substituting or supporting vocal expression. A gift of flowers has always been welcome in time of illness or bereavement. Joyous occasions such as weddings or birthdays offer other opportunities to share bouquets. Doesn't it give you an intense feeling of well-being to know that you might have brought out deep emotions of a loved one by such a simple act

Autumn Kimberly.
(Photo courtesy of
Yoder Brothers Inc.)

as giving them a flower? By enthusiastically sharing your emotions you can possibly stir a romantic and loving response in the recipient. This is one secret to success in relationships with others. Practice it until you become proficient at making others happy.

Culture

Zone 4

pH 6.5-7

Sun/Part Shade

**Height:
4 inches to 3
feet**

The Composite (or Daisy) family (Compositae) is a huge family of about 950 genera, including Artemisia, Aster, Calendula, Chrysanthemum, Dahlia, Echinacea, Gerbera, Liatris, Rudbechia, Santolia, and Zinnia. The more than 150 Chrysanthemum species are often aromatic annual or perennial herbs native mostly to Europe and Asia.

Several species include:

- Coccineum, a well-known Painted Daisy that grows from 1 to 3 feet high, has a summer bloom from which the pyrethrum insecticide is extracted.
- Leucanthemum, a self-seeding Oxeye Daisy, flowers April to June, earlier than Shasta Daisies, and can grow to 3 feet high.
- Weyrichii, a Daisy mum that grows to 1 foot in height, has good red color and blooms all summer and into the fall. This mum multiplies quickly in warm regions and in sandy soil.

These aromatic plants are available in every color but blue and most do well in containers. Their long-lasting blossoms make them a favorite of florists.

Opposite: _Sarah._ *(Photo courtesy of Yoder Brothers Inc.)* **Right: _Fructesceus._** *(Photo courtesy of Michael A. Dirr, Ph.D.)*

Gardening TIPS

Growing
- Easy to moderately difficult to grow, Chrysanthemums enjoy a good humus-rich, well-drained soil in full sun. Some will need more shade in the South.
- Chrysanthemums benefit from frequent application of fertilizer.
- Mulch to protect from weeds and to help keep moisture constant.
- Unlike many plants, mums can be transplanted while in bloom.

Pruning
- Frequent pinching of tips early in the growing season is necessary to keep young plants compact and bushy, otherwise staking may be required. Cease pinching in midsummer or when the plants begin to flower.
- Thin the plants 12 to 24 inches apart for best blooms.
- Remove faded blossoms regularly.

Propagation
- These plants can be propagated by seed, division, or cuttings.
- Sow seeds in early spring in order for the plants to flower around October.
- Divide plants in the spring to improve old beds and start new ones.
- After the last frost, buy rooted cuttings from nurseries for planting.

Availability
OF NOVEMBER BIRTHFLOWER OF THE LANDSCAPE™

Since hard frost may come in October in northern areas, it is impossible to have a late-blooming mum flower outside of a greenhouse in November. Southern areas, however, will have a profusion of mums blooming. Northerners can have earlier blooming varieties in their yards, or potted florist mums, and greenhouse plants inside.

Generally, a white mum, Alaska, is available September 15 through December 15. An order of 48 cushion mums usually brings you 12 each of 4 colors: red, yellow, bronze, and pink. Indicate your preferences on the order form.

To learn of collectors or flower shows in your area or to meet other people interested in
CHRYSANTHEMUMS, *contact:*

National Chrysanthemum Society, Inc.
10107 Homar Pond Drive
Fairfax Station, VA 22039-1650
(703) 978-7981

Above: *(Photo courtesy of Michael A. Dirr, Ph.D.)* **Right:** *(Photo courtesy of Yoder Brothers Inc.)*

CHAPTER XII

❧ CAMELLIA ❧

December Birthflower of the Landscape™

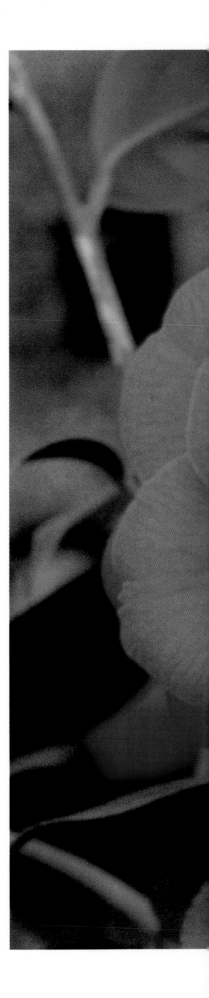

If we have no mountains to boast of, we have the sea, which is ever enjoyable, and we have Camellias. . . .

QUEEN VICTORIA, 1845

CHINA IS THE HOME of the Camellia, as are the neighboring lands of India, Burma, Korea, Formosa, and Japan. The native habitat of this vibrant plant is the picturesque world of misty valleys and gently sloping hillsides with sparse forests. In such places confident Camellias grow to become moss-covered trees reaching over 30 feet high with smooth, gray trunks more than a foot thick. These aristocrats of the garden were so sacred to the Chinese that it was forbidden to gather seeds or take even a single cutting.

The genus Camellia is named for a Jesuit priest, George Kamel (1661-1706), who traveled throughout China and the Philippines collecting plants. It is unclear whether Kamel brought seeds of the Camellia to Europe, but we do know that the first plants in England bloomed in Lord Petre's garden at Thornden Hall in Essex in 1739. Unfortunately, the Camellia soon disappeared from England, probably due to general ignorance in how to care for it. In

Mathotian. (Photo courtesy of Michael A. Dirr, Ph.D.)

1792, however, John Slater of the famed East India Company brought four Camellias to England and successfully reintroduced the beautiful flower to that country.

The plant's dislike of lime, its love of fog, and its requirements of shade, shelter, and a well-drained site are indicative of the precise needs of the Camellia. Maybe it is these requirements that have always made them more expensive than many other plants, more cherished and pampered as a garden plant, and surrounded with a more sophisticated and confident aura. In the southeastern United States and on the Pacific coast, especially, Camellias are popular as ornamental outdoor shrubs.

The December/Camellia MYSTIQUE

Exploring Honest Optimistic

In December, what can be more cheerful than the unexpected burst of color of a Camellia contrasting vividly with the gray of a winter landscape? This welcome accent mirrors the optimistic and expectant attitude of a person who is born in the month when these plants "burst wide open" with enthusiastic color. The exciting color splash of the Camellia also represents the exploring, adventurous nature of the December born. Straightforward and honest, these individuals brighten the world around them with their vivid presence, and the equally bright blossoms of their Birthflower is one of the things they yearn to share. In their hopeful and confident manner, they encourage others to explore and magnify the positive aspects of being born in December.

To give someone a Camellia or a gift with the Camellia pictured on it is to pass on to them these traits of honesty, happiness, cheerfulness, and love of adventure. The longer they are able to keep the image of this tender, beautiful flower visible to them, the stronger these traits will become a part of their personality. The more often they think of these attributes, the more they will observe the qualities of reliability, genuineness, and authenticity within themselves.

Morray Johnstone.
(Photo courtesy of
Michael A. Dirr, Ph.D.)

Shay Dean.

(Photo courtesy of

Marvin Jernigan.)

Culture

Zone 7

pH 6-7

Part Shade

Height: Up to 25 feet

The Tea family (Theaceae) has about 25 genera of mostly tropical, evergreen trees and shrubs, including Camellia and Cleyera.

The 80 or more Camellia species include:

- Japonica, the common Camellia or Japanese Camellia, is an evergreen shrub or small tree that can grow 20 to 25 feet high, with flowers 3 to 5 inches wide, ranging from dark red to white. Several hundred cultivars exist, with many new cold-hardy cultivars in development and beginning to show on the market.
- Sasanqua, an evergreen shrub that grows 6 to 10 feet high, has smaller leaves and flowers and an earlier bloom than Japonica.
- Sinensis is the tea plant, and is economically the most important Camellia. This species grows to 4 to 6 feet high and blooms early to late autumn. This species provides white blossoms 1 to $1^{1}/_{2}$ inches wide and is less sensitive to cold, heat, and drought than the Japonica and Sasanqua Camellias. Its leaves provide the world with one of its most popular beverages.

Occasionally lightly fragrant, Camellias offer large, often double flowers in shades of white, pink, red, and combinations of these colors. Slow-growing plants that produce flowers while still very young, Camellias come in so many combinations of form and color in flowers and have attracted such great interest that there are societies dedicated specifically to this perennial. Members are people who have a special affinity for the flower and hold annual conventions to show off new cultivars of superlatives — biggest, smallest, color never seen, new combinations of colors, doubles, etc. Often they are hobbyists who collect and propagate, grow bonsai and tree forms, and share their enthusiasm for this wonderful flower.

Gardening TIPS

Growing

- Camellias prefer well-drained soil, in some shade, that is moist, acidic, and high in organic content.
- Mulch well to maintain even moisture.
- Place in a spot protected from winter wind.
- Take care not to plant too deep (see Introduction, page 10).
- Fertilize with a formula especially for Camellias or acid-loving plants, following the directions on the package of fertilizer.
- Supplemental fertilizing with Epsom salts (magnesium sulfate) helps increase bloom size and number.

- In colder climates, they can be grown indoors in containers, with a temperature of 50° to 60° Fahrenheit required during the flowering season. Watch for chlorosis, or yellowing of leaves, which results from iron deficiency, and treat with a fertilizer supplemented with iron derived from pyrite and iron sulfate.

Pruning
- Espaliér (drive nails into wall and tie on plants to spread out flat) on easterly, westerly, or sheltered north-facing wall for a nice effect.
- It is better to wait until after the plants have flowered to shape or prune, however, you can prune anytime.

Propagation
- Plant hormone-treated cuttings taken from current season's growth in summer, or graft untreated cuttings onto suitable rootstock.

Availability

OF DECEMBER BIRTHFLOWER OF THE LANDSCAPE™

 Northern areas must grow this delicate beauty inside in containers to enjoy December flowers year after year. Camellia bushes and trees are breathtaking to those unfamiliar with this vibrant plant. It is surprisingly easy to make the effort to grow something this beautiful.

Because of soil restrictions in California, Oregon, Washington state, and New Mexico, we cannot ship containerized plants to these states. Though it is difficult to do, our preferred method is to ship bare root or liners when plant material is available. We will do our best to meet your needs.

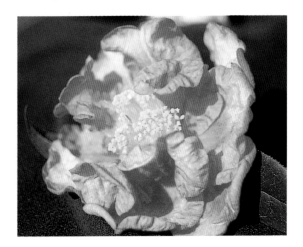

To learn more about this flower and to meet others interested in growing CAMELLIAS, *contact:*

American Camellia Society
1 Massie Lane
Fort Valley, Georgia 31030
(912) 967-2358

Opposite: *Mrs. Dan Nathen.*

Above: *Louise Gerbing.*

(Photos courtesy of Marvin Jernigan.)

Birthflowers of the Landscape™
PHOTO CONTEST

Commercial Landscaping Network, Inc. (CLN) is proud to sponsor its first of three (1998, 1999, 2000) United States of America annual Birthflowers of the Landscape™ Photo Contest. Winners will have their photographs published in subsequent printings of this book, *Birthflowers of the Landscape*™.

Who Can Enter?

The contest is open to anyone who submits a 5" x 7" photograph of any of the 12 Birthflowers of the Landscape™ that is judged by CLN staff to be suitable for framing.

Photo credit will be given when the book is next published. All rights to the negative and photo copyright will be assumed by CLN upon the acceptance of the prize money by the winners. You may enter as many times as you like.

What Prizes Can I Win?

1. Cash prizes of $35.00 will be given for 5 winning entries in each of the 12 Birthflower categories. These 60 entries will be published in future editions of *Birthflowers of the Landscape*™. An additional $65.00 (making the total $100.00) will be given to the Best of Show of each of the 12 categories.
2. Judging will be done and awards will be given according to the sole opinion of the officers and directors of CLN. Their decision will be final.
3. Prizes will be awarded at a CLN presentation on September 15 of each year. Entries must be received before September 1 of each year. All photos not winning a prize may be picked up within 30 days. All photos not claimed within this time frame will be discarded or returned to sender in their self-addressed stamped envelope.

Categories

1. January — Narcissus

2. February — Forsythia

3. March — Azalea
  (rhododendron)

4. April — Iris

5. May — Rose

6. June — Hydrangea

7. July — Crape Myrtle
  (lagerstroemia)

8. August — Phlox

9. September — Canna

10. October — Daylily
  (hemerocallis)

11. November —
  Chrysanthemum

12. December — Camellia

We want to show off each Birthflower of the Landscape™ to its best possible advantage —whether as a single bloom or in masses of group plantings. Choice of background is an artistic decision left to the photographer entrant.

Category Awards: Entrants should select any species or cultivar from the list to the left to photograph:

Dates and Deadlines

Entries may be sumitted anytime before September 1 of each year. It is not necessary that an entry be for the Birthflower of the month when the photograph is submitted.

Entries may be mailed to: Commercial Landscaping Network Photo Contest
P.O. Box 1885-601
Milledgeville, Georgia 31061

Rules

1. All photographs must be the work of the entrant and must be originals. No photographs of photographs permitted.

2. An Official Entry Form (below) must accompany each entry. Negatives should be in a protective cover.

3. All winning photographs and negatives will become property of CLN upon payment of prize money.

4. On the back of each print, *lightly* print your name, address, home or business phone number, category entered, and the title of your photograph. Include the botanical name of the flower. CLN reserves the right to change the category if a photograph is entered incorrectly.

5. CLN will exercise care with all entries but is not responsible for any damage to or loss of any photos or negatives.

Official Photo Contest Entry Form

Date:_____

Name:_____

Address:_____

City:_____ State:_____ Zip:_____

Home Phone:_____

Business Phone:_____

List all prints you are entering:

Category	Botanical Name
_____	_____
_____	_____
_____	_____
_____	_____
_____	_____
_____	_____
_____	_____
_____	_____
_____	_____
_____	_____
_____	_____

Total # of prints entered: _____

I CONFIRM THAT I HAVE READ THE RULES OF THE CPN SPONSORED LANDSCAPE BIRTHFLOWER CONTEST AND HAVE COMPLIED WITH SAID RULES.

Signature:_____

(OR GUARDIAN IF UNDER 18)

Return form to CPN, Photo Contest, P.O. Box 1885-601, Milledgeville, Georgia 31061

Free Birthflowers of the Landscape™ Plants
GUIDE AND APPLICATION

The following is a guide for obtaining FREE Birthflowers of the Landscape™ Plants—a more than $3,000.00 value—merely by sponsoring and completing a planned community service project.

In October of 1998, 1999, and 2000 Commercial Landscaping Network will agree to make available to ten tax-exempt civic organizations (i.e. Kiwanis, Boy Scouts, Garden Clubs, etc.) the equivalent of the recommended number of plants to landscape three residential lots. The Birthflowers are for the organization to use in the landscaping beautification of a local park or public-use area. This offer is limited to one allotment per city or town located in the U.S.

The organization will be required to complete the application form on page 121 and submit an acceptable written "Plan of Action" detailing who, what, when, where, how, and how much will be required to complete the project in each of five areas:

1. Project promotion: i.e. newspaper or radio public service announcements to be made before, during, and after project.
2. Landscape plan drawing detailing what plants will be planted, including where and how soil will be prepared.
3. Installation or planting plants. This is the fun part. You can make new friends and get to know your community, neighbors, and fellow members of your organization better, all while doing something worthwhile for your own community. Contacts and friends made this way are invaluable.
4. Maintenance agreement. This includes getting plants established, pruning, keeping weeds out, keeping mulch and fertilizer applied, and watering.
5. Fund-raising project for the purchasing of needed mulch.

contact: Commercial Landscaping Network
Free Landscape Plants Application
P.O. Box 1885-601
Milledgeville, Georgia 31061

Application for Free Landscape Plants

Date:_____

Name of Organization:_____

      IRS 501 Tax exemption number (if available):_____

Address:_____

City:_____ State:_____ Zip:_____

Name and title of Organizational head:_____

(CLUB PRESIDENT, DISTRICT OFFICER, DIRECTOR, OR OTHER PERSON

IN OFFICIAL CAPACITY TO SPEAK FOR THE ORGANIZATION)

Signature of organizational head :_____

                    Phone:_____

Name and title of Approving Local Official:_____

(PARKS DIRECTOR, MAYOR, COUNTY COMMISSIONER, OR OTHER PERSON IN OFFICIAL CAPACITY

WHO IS RESPONSIBLE FOR APPROVING WORK ON THE PUBLIC PROPERTY DESIGNATED)

Signature of Approving Local Official:_____

                    Phone:_____

Name of Chairperson:_____

Signature of Chairperson:_____

                    Phone:_____

Return form to CPN, Free Landscape Plants, P.O. Box 1885-601, Milledgeville, Georgia 31061

Bibliography

Austin, Alfred. American Hydrangea Society newsletter. January 1997, p. 7. (Vol. 3, Issue 1)

Buchanan, Rita, and Roger Holmes, eds. *Taylor's Guide to Gardening in the South.* New York: Houghton Mifflin Company, 1992.

Erhardt, Walter. *Hemerocallis: Daylilies.* Portland: Timber Press, 1992.

Haun, Jacqueline. Website: http://www.netonecom.net~jacq/poetry/forsythia.html

Heath, Brent and Becky. *Daffodils for American Gardens.* Washington, D.C.: Elliott & Clark Publishing, 1995.

Hudak, Joseph. *Gardening with Perennials Month by Month.* New York: Ademeter Press Book, 1976.

Kellaway, Deborah. *Irises and Other Flowers.* New York: Harry N. Abrams, 1995.

KÖhlein, Fritz. *Iris.* Portland: Timber Press, 1987.

L. H. Bailey Hortorium, Cornell University, staff. *Hortus Third: A Concise Dictionary of Plants Cultivated in the United States and Canada.* New York: Macmillan Publishing Company, 1976.

Lacy, Allen, ed. *The American Gardener: A Sampler.* New York: Farrar Straus Giroux, 1988.

Loewer, Peter. *A Year of Flowers.* Emmaus, Pennsylvania: Rodale Press, 1989.

Macoboy, Stirling. *The Colour Dictionary of Camellias.* Neutral Bay, New Zealand: Stirling Macoboy Books, 1992.

Mallet, Corinne. *Hydrangeas: Species and Cultivars.* Varengeville, France: Centre d'Art Floral, 1992.

Meredith Corporation, eds. *Better Homes and Gardens: Complete Guide to Gardening.* Des Moines, Iowa: Meredith Corporation, 1979.

Organic Gardening magazine, eds. *Q & A: Hundreds of Can-Do Answers to A Gardener's Toughest Questions.* Emmaus, Pennsylvania: Rodale Press, 1989.

Perry, Frances. *Flowers of the World.* New York: Crown Publishing, Inc., 1972.

Publications International. *Treasury of Gardening.* Lincolnwood, Illinois: Publications International, Ltd., 1994.

Randall, Harry and Alan Wren. *Growing Chrysanthemums.* Bromley, Kent: Christopher House Ltd., 1983.

Sackville-West, Victoria Mary. *Vita Sackville-West's Garden Book.* New York: Atheneum, 1968.

Schuler, Stanley. *The Gardener's Basic Book of Flowers.* New York: Simon and Schuster, 1974.

Stout, A. B. *Daylilies.* Sagaponack, New York: Sagapress, Inc., 1986.

Todd, Pamela. *Flora's Gems: The Little Book of Daffodils.* New York: Little, Brown and Company, 1994.

Warburton, Bee. *The World of Irises.* Wichita, Kansas: The American Iris Society, 1978.

Whittle, Michael Tyler. *Some Ancient Gentlemen.* New York: Taplinger Publishing Company, 1965.

Glossary

ACIDIC: The opposite of alkaline. Old, exhausted soil sometimes not well-drained contains carbonic, humic, tannic, and other acids. Add lime to make acid soils more neutral.

ALKALINE: The opposite of acidic. Associated with limestone country and "hard" water where there is not enough rain to wash away the alkali salts, leaving them to accumulate in the soil. Add aluminum sulfate or sulfur to make alkaline soils more neutral.

CULTIVAR: Cultivated variety of a plant (modern term).

DEADHEADING: Removing spent, dead blooms from the plant.

DIVIDING: Divide clumps of plants into smaller clumps with your hand or use a shovel. To divide rhizomes (fleshy underground roots), you will need a knife to cut them into small clumps. To allow these wounds to seal themselves, let the cut rhizomes air out for an hour or so. As a general rule, divide every three years (see Chart, page 14) to keep flowers looking good. Best time to divide is late fall.

ESPALIER: Term for a trellis, or lattice, on which a tree is trained to grow. The art is a practice for allowing maximum light and air, improving appearance.

FERTILIZER RATIO: A fertilizer with the labeled ratio of 5-10-15 consists of 5 parts nitrogen (to promote leaf or green growth), 10 parts phosphorus (to strengthen stems and help produce more flowers), and 15 parts potassium (to promote root growth and healthier plants). This is an oversimplification.

FORCING: Making plants grow and flower outside their natural seasons.

FRIABLE: Easily crumbled or pulverized soil allows the circulation of air to roots.

GRAFT/GRAFTED PLANTS: The beautiful flowering top part (scion) of one plant is made to unite with and grow upon the stronger root system, or the bottom part (stock), of another plant.

HARDENED OFF: Plants that have survived their first winter and can now be considered winter hardy.

HUMUS: Brown or black material resulting from decomposition of organic matter. The primary component of compost.

LIME: Limestone. Mostly calcium carbonate with some magnesium carbonate. Dolomitic limestone is used to reduce soil acidity or sourness.

LINERS: Term used by growers to denote very young and tender plants, less than a year old, which are grown in the field and in containers before being sold to the retail trade.

MULCH, MULCHING: Adding organic material (mulch) around plants and on top of the soil to retain moisture and maintain an even temperature, improving the environment of the plants in that soil. Mulch is the easiest to use and the best combatant for the three most troublesome things about gardening: watering, weeds, and insects.

pH BALANCE: Percent of hydrogen or hydrogen-iron activity in gram equivalents per liter. Values run from 0 to 14, and 7 represents neutrality. Numbers less than 7 denote increasing acidity and numbers greater than 7 denote increasing alkalinity.

RHIZOMES: Large, fleshy underground stems. A thick, bulbous rootstock that is not a true bulb. These are found in Iris and Canna.

ROOT ROT: Roots need air as well as water. If roots are planted too deep in soil and cannot get enough air, the roots will rot and die.

ROOTING, or HOOKING, or LAYERING: To multiply your plants, scratch or pull off bark from the tip of a branch and bend it to the ground. Hold the branch tip down by weighing it down into the soil with a stone or brick. The branch will quickly root and grow. This technique is commonly called "layering." Applying root hormone will help this process.

ROSE HIPS: Seed pods on a rose bush or rose tree.

Index

Acknowledgments

 To Judy Williamson, for editing, typing, reading, believing, supporting, praying, and . . . writing the mystique sections.

To Michael A. Dirr, Ph.D., for his encouragement and direction on this book.

To Barbara J. Clinton, Ph.D., and her Desktop Publishing Class at Georgia College for layout and design work on the author's original manuscript.

About the Author

 While an Eagle Scout as a teenager, Linton Wright McKnight developed an interest in nature that has continued to be major part of his life. In recent years he has often observed colorful flowers in the landscape, noting those requiring such low maintenance that they seem to thrive on neglect. This book is his opportunity to share those observations with others.

A graduate of the University of Georgia, McKnight owned and operated a jewelry store, ran his own landscaping business, and spent more than 20 years as a real estate broker specializing in the brokerage of farms and acreage. He lives in Milledgeville, Georgia.